DARN IT!

MAYBE I MISSED SOMETHING!

To Bean,

DARN IT!
MAYBE I MISSED SOMETHING!

Musings of a
Spiritually Challenged
Redneck

GLENN BERRY

Tate Publishing & *Enterprises*

Darn It! Maybe I Missed Something!
Copyright © 2010 by Glenn Berry. All rights reserved.

No part of this publication may be reproduced, stored in a retrieval system or transmitted in any way by any means, electronic, mechanical, photocopy, recording or otherwise without the prior permission of the author except as provided by USA copyright law.

The opinions expressed by the author are not necessarily those of Tate Publishing, LLC.

Published by Tate Publishing & Enterprises, LLC
127 E. Trade Center Terrace | Mustang, Oklahoma 73064 USA
1.888.361.9473 | www.tatepublishing.com

Tate Publishing is committed to excellence in the publishing industry. The company reflects the philosophy established by the founders, based on Psalm 68:11,
"The Lord gave the word and great was the company of those who published it."

Book design copyright © 2010 by Tate Publishing, LLC. All rights reserved.
Cover design by Leah LeFlore
Interior design by Lindsay B. Behrens

Published in the United States of America

ISBN: 978-1-61663-920-4
1. Religion / Christian Life / Men's Issues   2. Religion / Christian Life / General
10.08.23

TABLE OF CONTENTS

Preface. 7
Oh Boy! I'm Scared Now!. 9
I'm Not Sure If Heaven Is the Place for Me!. . . . 19
Since I Probably Won't Make It Anyway. 25
I Think I Know When He's Coming! 33
I Wonder If God's First Name Is Ohhhh?. 37
What Do You Mean "Jesus Is the
   Sweetest Name I Know"? 45
Oh Boy! This Heaven Thing Is a
   Whole Different Deal 53
Wow! God Understands Redneck English! 61
Maybe He Ain't a Schizo!. 71
I Still Ain't Liking the Idea of Fighting
   a Devil I Can't See!. 79
Is Hearing God As Easy As They Say? 87
Reckon What Would Happen If… 95

He Gives Me the Shivers!.	103
Working Together? Now I Can Do That!	111
I've Been Afraid to Ask These Questions!.	119
I Know Him. He's My Father!	127
I Am Amazed!.	135
The Way You See Him Is the Way You Will Serve Him!	145
Photo Gallery	151

PREFACE

In November of 2009, I made a brief trip back to Oklahoma. While visiting the area in which I was raised, I had opportunity to pass through most of the sites mentioned in this book. As I watched the Christmas parade in my old hometown, I was reminded of what a great place it is and what a good place it was to grow up. The people in that area—Chelsea, Vinita, Big Cabin, Foyil, Condry, to name a few—are the salt of the earth. They still live in a rural America that many will never have the privilege of knowing and understanding. During the parade, the main street of Chelsea, Oklahoma was lined with people. Children were walking up and down the street at will. Parents felt very secure. They knew that neighbor still looks after neighbor in this town. A very small girl rode in the parade mounted on a half-broke horse, and no one thought she was at risk in any way.

As I walked some of the old trails and thought back more than forty years, I had the writing of this book on my mind. The responsibility of a writer is very real to me. I know that when this book is printed, its words can never be retracted. The words will have their impact and will leave their impression on whoever might read them. This was very much on my mind as I visited one of the local churches on Sunday morning. As I spoke, I was aware that there were many in attendance who had served our Lord and Savior for more than forty years. That congregation represented hundreds of years of effort to do the best they could to follow Him. I feel a real need to give all of them credit where credit is due. Much of who I am today is the result of the efforts of those people in their service to God. Without their willingness to make that effort, I would never have started on the journey described in these pages.

In the best of Oklahoma tradition, I "tip my hat" to all those who have contributed their very best to enable me and many others to become more than we could have been through any other means. May the blessings of God be with them as they continue in their way of life.

OH BOY! I'M SCARED NOW!

Until now, I thought I was a regular guy. I liked to hunt, fish, and just generally ramble around the countryside where I was growing up. My family wasn't functional or dysfunctional. We didn't know much about those words in those days. We were just a family. Now I realize that it was quite dysfunctional to be part of a family like that. I guess I don't see how we are going to become victims like everyone else if we suppress all those bad memories. While it would probably be better for my mental health to find some reason to blame all this on my mom and dad—don't know what all *this* is, but it must be there—right now it really feels like God might be talking to me through this preacher I'm listening to.

We come to church all the time. Ever since I can remember, I've slept, whispered, and ignored the preacher; I've gotten myself in real trouble in church.

But, today, it's just different somehow. I'm not real sure what being saved means, but I'm pretty sure I need to get it done. I'm getting a mental picture of God here. I guess I just didn't settle down to realize it before, but I think I must be one of those sinners the preacher is talking about.

That hell thing is very scary. Oh yeah. I'm just like every other boy in this crowd. I'll never admit that out loud, but I am scared. Seems that if I haven't said some certain words, I am tottering on the very brink of hell. Just last week I had something like that happen. That old tree that fell across the wash up the hill a ways? I was walking across that and lost my balance. I was tottering. Just about fell into the blackberry bushes under that log. I don't like the idea of tottering over a lake of fire like that. I was kind of scared then, but this hell thing is really scary. It's probably my imagination, but I get this idea of God, fire in His eyes, retribution in His heart, preparing to cast me into this lake of fire. Yep. He's talking about me. I just know it because of this fear that is gripping me. It must be the fear of God I read about in my Sunday school lesson.

But I don't know about walking down that aisle. Everybody will be watching. They're not supposed to, but I know they do. I've done it. I always do it. If you cross your arms on the seat in front of you and lay your head down like you are praying, you can peek and see it all. If you sit far enough back you can even see most of those who raise their hands. Most of them are like me. They ain't walking up there! I've seen what happens when you walk up there. They all gather around you. Some whisper quietly. Others yell. But they are all looking at you. Nope—maybe next week.

One thing's for sure: now I know I am not just a regular guy. I am tottering on the brink of hell. To tell you the truth, I am afraid of God. But, if I act like I have been saved, they won't expect me to walk down that aisle. Besides that, I am emotional right now. I'm not used to that. I know real men don't cry, but I feel like crying. Guess I'd rather face God than face all those people if I cry.

I wonder if I could just talk to God. Maybe when I am roaming the countryside God and I could come to some understanding. I really would like to know Him. I'm not sure if I can. I am sure that I don't want to walk down that aisle and cry.

I begin to talk with God. I'm really surprised. It's like He talks back to me. I'm probably mistaken again. The reason I think so is that I am listening to what the preacher's saying now. I don't make a big deal out of it. Most folks probably can't tell, but I'm listening. I can't quite figure out what to do. I am learning a lot about what not to do, and that is a problem. Seems to me that everything I want to do I'm supposed to just stop it.

Darn it! Uh oh. I'm not supposed to say that, or even think it. It's just another form of cussing. The youth leader said so. I wonder what she thinks of some of the things I've heard her say when she's mad. But I guess I've missed something. In Sunday school class the teacher is always talking about how God loves us. Well, that's not completely true. Those teachers are always talking about how God loves the people in the Bible stories. I'm not sure God can like me. I've done a lot of things that I know are wrong. I've heard the preacher say so!

I really like some of those guys in the Bible stories, though. Samson! What a guy! I wonder if the Holy Spirit will ever come on me like that. Probably not. He was something special, I reckon. Like David. I can relate to him. Seems I'm always taking care of cows. I know they're not sheep, but it sure seems like a full-time job to me. I've tried the sling. Almost took out the windshield of Dad's truck. That would be bad, believe me. Then Granddad showed me how to make a "bean flip." Get a good green fork of hickory and cut some rubber out of an inner tube—they were still made out of rubber in those days. Carve a seat out of the tongue of an old work boot. Tie it all together with some more thin rubber cut from the inner tube and you'll have something that can be controlled. But I still couldn't hit within the width of a hair like David's men. Hit a tin can every time, but not with either hand! That darn—oops—hair seemed to move every time. Maybe David was something more special than me.

    I really want to be saved. I don't think about hell much anymore. I'm learning to tune out the preacher. I did listen to the messages on end times, though. Seems like eternity is a long way off. And all those sins—and it is a long list—are things that sound very interesting. Matter of fact, I'm trying out a lot of them. I didn't know about most of them until the preacher started hollering about them. Maybe I'm listening more than I think, but I still think I'm missing something. Sometimes I think about eternity. The way I understand it, eternity is out there somewhere. It's not touching my world today. Somehow it seems like something that I don't want to be a part of. The way my life is now is fun but scary. Most boys I know like to live like that.

    There is this thing in me that really likes the idea of being bad. All those things the preacher talked about, and Mom and Dad repeated over and over, seem so interesting. My experience with them shows that those things are fun and dangerous. I've done a lot of those things that seem to make God throw people in hell. Folks are always talking about sinning past your day of redemption. I'm not sure what that means, but I think I missed that day. I'm always feeling bad about what I'm doing, and then I get caught up in the excitement and end up doing it anyway. But, darn it, I still think I am missing something.

I love to read. It takes me into other worlds and adventures that I could never reach any other way. In my world TV is sin. A boy needs to read. Some of my books I hide up in the pasture. If Mom found them I would be in real trouble. I can escape to a world of adventure and a world of sin. I decided to read about Samson and David on my own. Why didn't anyone tell me about their sin? I'm not so interested in how they handled it, but in what they did and how they did it. Now I know I am missing something. These guys turned out okay, so I'm taking my chances, just like them. I've about got this eternity thing figured out anyway. I've proven to be indestructible. Things that would almost kill someone else haven't affected me much. Just the other day, I tied my little brother's wagon to the horn of my horse's saddle. Without thinking about the rattling and banging of the wagon behind him—he's a bit excitable on any day—I jumped in and hollered, "Get up! Hyah!" Did we ever go! He forgot all about, "Whoa!" If the wagon hadn't hit that old stump we would still be going. I finally caught up with him when the rope tangled with persimmon sprouts back in the woods. My mom can never know about this. I'm sure it would cause a heart attack if she finds out about this.

Darn It! Maybe I Missed Something!

Speaking of my mom, when we bought the farm, the previous owner left an old and unbroken mare for a few weeks. That horse fascinated me. Mom threatened me with cruel and unusual punishment if I tried to ride her. I really didn't intend to ride her, but I did want to tame her. Okay, the thought to ride her must have been back there somewhere, but I never would have admitted it! Just an admission like that could have provoked Mom to the cruel and unusual. I was just going to get that mare where I could pet her. Through great effort and long hours of following her all over the farm, I finally got her to allow me to touch her. Then she allowed me to groom her with a bunch of sage grass. Then I could put my arm over her neck. I was enjoying that horse.

I just had to try it. No. I wasn't going to ride her; just put my weight on her withers. I draped my body over and she jumped, throwing me to the ground. No big deal. She could have stomped me, but she didn't. A few hundred more tries and I could drape my body over her and she wouldn't even flinch. Somehow the thought just invaded my consciousness. I could ride her. With little effort I just hopped aboard. I was wrong. She wasn't broken. In two jumps she was running flat out. I could hang on or fall off into blackberry bushes. If I had it to do over, I would have chosen the blackberries. I could have lied my way out of the scratches—I was getting good at that by now.

That mare ran straight to the barn. And was she ever fast! There was a long hill just before the barn area. While running down that hill, she decided to tuck her head and buck. She missed her calling. She should have been in rodeo! I went straight over her head and right in front of her running hooves. Now anyone who knows much about horses knows that most of them will automatically step over and around a body. She didn't touch me with a single hoof. She didn't need to. The hard sandstone of northeastern Oklahoma took care of all the cuts and bruises that were necessary.

But, back to my mom. Wouldn't you know it? She was at the sink, washing breakfast dishes, looking out the window when the horse came over the hill. At first she was amused—I didn't know this until I was thirty-five—but then I went over that horse's head. She came out of that house with retribution in mind. Need I say more? The bruises from the fall seemed minor at that moment.

Through these and many more incidents—in which I was mostly innocent—I came to believe that I could live through about anything. So, I was not very worried about dying before the Lord came back. Since I thought being saved was boring and without fun, I needed to figure out when He was coming. I figured if I could make it until I was about twenty-one or so, I could get saved and slide under the wire, or the trumpet, whichever. In my mind salvation had become all about staying out of hell. Life was about trying everything, living dangerously (and it was dangerous to disobey Mom and Dad), and rising to the thrill of challenge. Obviously, I was missing something.

I'M NOT SURE IF HEAVEN IS THE PLACE FOR ME!

By now you have gotten an idea of how I grew up. In one sense a bit wild. At the same time very structured and confined. I had free run of about three or four sections of land. We only owned a small portion of that, but neighbors were kind and allowed us to roam all over as long as we closed gates and didn't bother the cows too much. As a result I was a guy who loved the outdoors, wide-open places, and a lot of activity. All of creation was a wonder to me, and I have never lost the wonder. As a boy I spent hours beside the creek watching the fish, small animals, and nature in general.

The structured and confined part was in the area of religion—it was religion, not relationship. When the doors of the church were open, we were there. All the chores at home had to be finished and schoolwork done, but we were at church every chance. There is nothing really wrong with that until it is attached to your salvation. And believe me, it was attached. And then we always had to consider sin. It was always with us. In every message. In every conversation. Salvation seemed to be personal, but I wasn't sure that it had anything to do with a relationship with God. If I had it right, salvation mostly depended on the things I did. I sure hoped I had missed something. By this time I was doing a lot of stuff, and most of it was not acceptable to God. That was personal. He would never accept a guy like me.

One of the deciding factors for me is the picture that is evolving in my mind about heaven. Seems that almost everyone has a different idea of what it is like and how you get there. For some, heaven is a bunch of mansions. The song talked about a gold mansion with silver lining. It also seemed that there wasn't much order there. Those mansions must be clustered around some throne? Couldn't be that many mansions. Also, I'll be living in this thing by myself. I guess Jesus has got one of them. Another song says that I want mine built next door to His. Just an observation here, and don't forget this is from a spiritually challenged redneck; but it seems to me there won't be room for very many mansions that close. I've helped build a lot of houses, and there are not many "next-door" places around any house I've ever seen.

Another song gets closer to my desires. "Just build me a cabin in a corner of gloryland." That is close, but still no cigar. I guess I shouldn't mention cigars while talking about heaven. But you should know they will make you real sick the first few times you smoke them. Don't ask me how I know. I'm still deciding if I want to go to heaven and don't want to be ruled out. And then all those songs and testimonies about streets of gold. You would have to be real careful how you walked on that. I'm still not convinced about the flying they talk about, although that would keep you off the gold with your dirty feet. Most folks I know would be out in the street with a hammer and chisel.

And then there's another picture that comes to mind. Eternity—I still haven't figured out when it starts, but I know it don't end—spent around a throne playing harps. I tried the steel guitar for a few years. That's cool, but a harp? For eternity? I wouldn't even like to listen to that, let alone play it myself. I'm probably missing something, but I think that being bored for eternity would nearly drive me crazy. If I had to listen to all that harp music for very long I just might wind up in the state mental hospital. That is closer to Vinita, Oklahoma, than it is to heaven.

I really don't feel good about this. I do want to know God. I do want to be saved. I'm reminded in every service about hell and about the coming nuclear explosion that will be just after the rapture (about three and one half years after) with peoples' eyeballs melting in their heads and skin peeling off their bones. Yes, sir, I do want to be saved. Although, part of me snickers and says, "I guess I wouldn't see it with my eyeballs melting." Darn it! I guess I missed something! I'm becoming more and more convinced that salvation is not an option for me. Every time some high-energy preacher comes through, I'm praying. Just trying to get some fire insurance, but in my heart, nothing's happening. God is just too demanding. It seems impossible for me to keep all the rules.

When I think of the rules, I'm pretty sure I understand what is happening. The rules change according to what the rule makers want to happen. Me and my cousins—my cousins and I (see I do know how, I just don't do it much) play war a lot. If my mom found out the way we play it, she would have a cow. You think that ain't possible? Then you don't know Oklahoma moms. Back to the cousins. We could speculate about Mom for a long time. We play with BB guns. Rules are that you can't shoot above the waist. That rule changes if you can't see anything below the waist. Sometimes you have to shoot the chest or arms so the other one will jump and you can keep the rules. And even if you do strictly keep the rules, this game ain't safe. If you know boys at all you know where they aim. And we spend a lot of time shooting. Our BB guns are accurate because we know how they shoot. I'm surprised we didn't all sire pockmarked kids. By the way, when you are hit by a BB, it looks a lot like an inflamed chigger bite or the measles. Either excuse will help Mom understand. But remember, the measles thing will only work once, and that is only if you haven't had the measles. Another thing. Shotgun pellets are harder to explain even if they are below the waist, especially when one of the cousins has to dig them out for you. Thank God for pocket knives! Makes it hard to sit normal in church, though. (Don't ask me how I know, but I hear you can suffer from those same pellets if you get too close to the wrong watermelon patch.) So, when from Sunday to Wednesday the rules seem to change, I understand. Someone wants something to happen that is not happening, or they don't want to start another war before they heal up from the last one. Perfectly understandable, but it truly does make it hard to keep up with the rules.

Sometimes when I am wandering around in the woods I am wishing I could get it all settled. Problem is that this stuff—things that break the rules—seems to be getting to be a part of me. It's weird, but the fact that I'm breaking a rule seems to make it more fun, challenging. Not only that, but my ability to break the rules and get by with it is making me something of a celebrity among the youth in our church. Dad is a little amused by some of it. Mom would like to prove that I'm guilty. I think she might have capital punishment in mind. If she proves it, Dad will get on board. I know he won't kill me, but I also know I'll probably wish I was dead. Now that is motivation to keep it covered up. I'm getting pretty good at being a double agent. I got that from some of the books that I have stashed in that tree. By now I know quite a lot about being the quiet, hardworking kid when I am in certain company. "Certain company" means those who are likely to tell my parents. That is a definition from the original language. But, when it is unlikely to get back home—everything is a gamble—then I do like to have fun.

SINCE I PROBABLY WON'T MAKE IT ANYWAY

I just can't. I don't see any way. It does keep coming back to my mind. By now, my whole thought process has changed. It's not about having a personal walk with God that changes me. It is about what has become fact to me. There seems to be nothing about me that can get to heaven—if I wanted to go. If I think about it, I get scared. How can I argue with God? I have been taught about how God worked all the miracles of the Old and New Testaments. If you mention a Bible story, I can tell you the superhero aspect of every one. I know about Sodom and Gomorrah. I am properly in awe of a God like that. He is one butt-kicking God. The Philistines knew that He used His chosen people to defeat them. In all the stories—at least the way they are told—there is one acceptable leader and then a bunch of chosen people who are never able to live up to being chosen. If those leaders didn't go to God for them, they would be wiped out. I just know I'm in one of those wipe-out categories. I know it. You can get there just by complaining. Or if you are a woman, by wearing a pair of jeans or some make-up.

How can I ever know a God like that? I know the argument. There is the sacrifice of Jesus, and I am grateful for that. But I keep getting reminded of the changing of the rules. In some messages, for a minute or two, it looks like the sacrifice of Jesus changed some things. But we always get back to the rules. What *can* I do? I know all about what I *cannot* do, although the list does keep changing. I am getting this mix of Old and New Testament, but there seems to be a major difference. The leaders I am listening to don't seem to be anywhere near going to God on my behalf. Jesus did all of that—and I am grateful—but I am still so tied up with rules that I can't get to know Him.

I still feel as if God knows more than I want Him to know about me. Jesus is presented as another of those superheroes that is somehow untouched by real life. I struggle. Don't you? I want to do some things that are not accepted in the rules. I don't do some things that are demanded by the rules. Then the rules change. Beards were accepted on Jesus. I reckon He made it to heaven. After all, He is up there building a mansion for you—not me, it seems, but for you.

Darn It! Maybe I Missed Something!

By now, I've begun building some things. I know about power tools, tool belts, and all that stuff. It seems that what Jesus learned in the carpenter shop is being put to good use. Even with supernatural ability it's going to take some time to get them mansions all built. Now, I'm really not liking what I'm thinking about those mansions. Subdivisions, cookie-cutter mansions, maybe even some low-performance housing? Naw, it couldn't be like that. My mind is continuing to be twisted by my redneck lifestyle! Back to the point, I don't like to shave. I have a beard. Just the other evening Sister Bucketmouth cornered me in the back of the church—yeah, I'm still going from time to time—and told me that my beard was going to send me straight to hell! If she only knew how hard I was laughing inside—I've been taught not to laugh at old, prophetic women. My mind is twisted and vivid. I see the Monopoly game of life. Do not collect a mansion. Do not expect a second chance. Go directly to hell. In my thinking that is funny, but I really don't want to pursue that thought. Also, I'm dumb enough to think the pastor might enjoy this story as well, so I tell him. He soberly responds, "I've intended to talk to you about that!" I guess I missed something in the Bible. Rules have changed since Jesus.

See how messed up I am? If I think deeply about God, it really scares me. For an Oklahoma country boy, it is hard to admit something scares me. But

God? I can feel Him. Sometimes I even think I hear Him—now that is challenging because I'm pretty sure He don't like me. But I can't see Him! He has proven how powerful He is. People I respect have convinced me that God is mad at me. I've heard about that Jonathan guy who talks about sinners in the hands of an angry God. It's probably best if I just don't think about it. Remember? I know by now when He is coming. I'll stop this sinning business in time to figure it all out. I've heard about those deathbed confessions. I'll reserve one of them. No matter how hard I try though, something gets to me. I guess it's God. When it gets quiet and I'm not otherwise occupied, here come those thoughts. By now I'm learning to stay occupied, very occupied. I still don't know why God won't leave me alone if He don't like me. Maybe this is a preview of hell. Naw, it can't be. No fire involved in this.

    I don't want to think about this. To stay away from it I need to be busy. Some of this sinning is a lot of fun. Since I don't have much, if any, chance of going to heaven anyway, I might as well get on with it. The way the religious folks talk about sin makes it sound interesting. I always chuckle remembering testimony services. Most of them seemed like commercials for sin. They laugh and talk with no small amount of pride about the awful things God delivered them from twenty or thirty years ago. The rules have changed since then. God is much less likely to deliver people now. He

Darn It! Maybe I Missed Something!

is much more likely to smash you in judgment. There I go thinking again. I told you I am messed up. Other testimonies seem to glorify Satan. "The devil's been after me all week. Bless His holy name!" I laughed right out loud at that one. My dad got involved in that little mistake. I didn't make it again. Seems that he did not think it was funny. But I know him. I'm betting he laughed when he really thought about it. Anyhow, I've just got to try some of that stuff they giggle about when we have church dinners.

One preacher makes a statement that bothers me. "Sin will keep you longer, cost you more, and take you further than you ever intended." That is scary because I'm experiencing it now. In the beginning it was a lot of fun to steal cherry vodka out of the case my older cousin kept in his closet. Or small amounts of the "medicinal" bourbon my uncle kept on his bedside table. And he needed quite a bit of medicine. Nobody ever missed a half pint or so. My cousin and I seemed to have a lot of flu in those years. You know, headaches, vomiting, and so on. And our parents never caught on to the smell. Oh, and you talk about fun. Did you know that a watermelon will absorb almost a quart of extra liquid? A small plug cut out of the rind and *glug, glug,* in it goes! Just slip the plug right back in and you've got a real surprise for someone. Even at a youth group watermelon party! Don't ask me how I know! And, yes there's more. A pint of pure grain alcohol slipped into the party punch also makes youth group interesting. To this day no one who was in charge knows why the youth had so much fun at some of those parties. Not all the youth, but some.

I never intended for this stuff to take me into some of these areas. Things I would have been afraid to do have now become normal. I'm refusing to think about what it means to be accepted in the kingdom of God. Even at a very young age I have become twisted in my thinking, focused on doing the things that have been presented as unacceptable. Something has developed in me that is not the kingdom of God. I find that I prefer to live this way. I can stay busy in the sinning business, and God rarely has the opportunity to get into my thinking. By now I have become a person that Christians who truly know my lifestyle do not dare to talk to—at least most of them. I know enough of the Bible to twist them around when they start to quote. My refusal to follow their rules makes them angry and confused. Mostly because my arrogant responses force them to think. They think they might be missing something.

They don't know that it is all a façade. I'm really not as tough as they think. When God can get me to think I do get miserable. My arrogant, disrespectful response to their Bible thumping is just to get them off my back. I do not want to think about it! But there are some people that continue to get through. I know their lives. I've watched them for years. They truly live what they believe. They are just different.

I was talking to one of those folks one day. We weren't talking about anything in particular. In the middle of asking how I was getting along she said, "How are you living?" Without waiting for a response she said, "I've been living for Jesus a long time. If I knew there was no heaven, I would still want to live this way." Another said to me, "Glenn, what are you going to do about Jesus?" There were no arrogant responses or any twisted Bible verses that could help me there. I had no answers and was forced into thinking. How did they know what to say? Why could they get under my sinful skin when others had pounded me with Bible verses and sinners' prayers with no response? Darn it! I guess I'm missing something! But I cannot allow myself to think about it. God don't like me. I've done almost all those things that are on His list.

I THINK I KNOW WHEN HE'S COMING!

I know I am not the sharpest knife in the drawer. I think about things too much. It seems that I just worry a thought like a dog works on a bone—now that is good Oklahoma English. It seems I am always working to find out more and more about things that other people just take as solid truth. Knowing this about myself has helped me understand some of the things the preachers have said about prophecy. I know it is hard to digest, but I'm guessing the prophets didn't say what they were really thinking so we would be busy figuring it out. Since we're so busy, that will probably keep us from sinning. It doesn't really work for me. By now, I'm pretty sure that nothing will keep me from doing all those things on the sin list.

Whoever came up with those end times charts had to be smart. All those little pictures and arrows amaze me. I'm betting the man that came up with all that didn't sin for most of his life. 'Cause he was a busy man, see? They make my head spin when all the explaining is going on. I sure am glad when the preacher finally gets to that part where he says, "Now, what the writer was trying to say is…" Every time I've been wondering about that for an hour or so. By the time he gets there I'm ready to take what he says as gospel. Anyone who can remember all those dates and times and arrows must have a direct connection to God. Now we know what the prophets were really saying. I wonder why they didn't just say it? I guess I'm missing something.

I figured out that Jesus was coming back very close to the year 2000. Which meant I had some time to sin—well, at least to live like I wanted to. But then this guy came by and said that the Jewish calendar was different than our Gregorian calendar. They seem to think that we lost six or seven years. Probably seven, because that is a holy number. Why is it a holy number? Haven't you read the Book? Well, at the very least listen to some preachers; they will tell you that numbers are important in the Bible. The Bible don't say so, but remember; they have a direct line to God. Now I'm in more of a mess. It seems I'm going to have to live by the rules seven years earlier than I thought. This could be very difficult if that Jewish calendar is wrong. I'm having trouble with just six or seven days of living by the rules. However, if it means I can miss hell, I'll surely try. Oh man, this is hard! I think I am missing something.

I'm reading some very interesting books. All about end times. The very idea makes me shiver. I found this big, thick book about God's plan for man. Most of it is filled with list after list of scripture references, but the words in between are interesting. I follow through some of those lists. Now I know I am not a scholar. Actually, in the minds of some, I am more dangerous than that. I am a thinker. What I am thinking is this. This guy starts with an idea. Then he sets out to prove that idea. It appears to me that he will do about anything with Bible verses to make his point, prove his doctrine. But in one sense he really catches my attention. The Bible really says that days are like years and years are like days. Not exactly like that, but something to that effect. Now that bothers me. I'm thinking that Jesus felt some of the same thing when He said that only the Father knows the day and the hour. Maybe all this time spent figuring on this subject isn't so good. Might just be a waste.

That ornery thing in me rears up. A day is as a thousand years, a thousand years is as a day. In that case I reckon I'm about a gazillion years old. Or maybe I'm not born yet. Or maybe I'm already dead and this is a foresight thing. Now I know all that is not true, but a young man's mind is not always in strict submission to the reality of the moment. One thing I'm pretty sure of, if I'm going to get any serious sinning done, I need to get on with it.

Now the preacher is saying something that seems different to me. He's agreeing with what the Bible says. No man knows the day nor the hour. I know it says that. I've read it and wondered about it. That means that all this stuff about when the end will come is a waste of time. He might come any time. Oh man. I've got to find out what it really means to know Him. For a guy who has decided he won't think about it, I sure am spending a lot of time trying to figure it out. Deep inside I really want to know God. Not just about Him. I want to *know* Him. But I'm pretty sure He don't want anything to do with the likes of me. After all, I can't even remember all the things on the list, let alone to not do them.

Anyway, right now it looks like God will drop the hammer anytime. That trumpet is gonna blow. Maybe today. They can get excited about that at church, but it just scares me. There might be some room, though. He's talking about a tribu … tribula … anyway a whole lot of trouble that is coming. They say we will be forewarned by a beginning of sorrows—whatever that means. I'm not counting on recognizing anything I can't even spell.

I WONDER IF GOD'S FIRST NAME IS OHHHH?

I never did finish telling you the story about the horse and the little red wagon. Even now, it seems like only yesterday. I'm in the wagon, and the horse is running faster every jump. Then I realize I have no control. The reins are tied with just the right looseness around the saddle horn. The horse is getting more and more scared every time the wagon hits the ground. Then I see that stump coming.

I had tied the rope to the front axle assembly of the wagon and folded the tongue back into the wagon. When I stood beside the wagon—before getting in— it seemed like an excellent idea. I thought it would give me some control. I was wrong. Those wagons just ain't designed for control at high speeds. Every time I pulled that tongue one way or the other, that wagon tilted crazily or whipped from side to side. Now I know why I've seen so many of these things wrecked at the bottom of hills. This is not good, but what do you do? If I jump off, my cousin will laugh his head off. He had promised to ride the second ride. Now that I think about it, he's a lot smarter than we give him credit for.

Anyhow, we're on the move. I reached the point of no return several yards ago. Then I see that old stump coming up. It's not very high and the horse isn't afraid of it at all. In the past I have ridden him over it on purpose because he jumps every time. In my mind I think I'm training him to eventually jump a fence. That did not work, but that's another story. That stump is coming and from my perspective in the wagon I know we ain't going to clear that stump, the horse is not going to go around it, and it is not likely the wagon is going to jump it. It probably will not launch over it just because the horse does, either.

Well, we hit it. Or, should I say the wagon hit it. The horse cleared it pretty well. The rope held on and tore the tongue and wheel assembly right off that wagon. I rolled and tumbled a bit, but now I am concerned about the horse. The wheel assembly off that wagon is hitting the ground every twenty or thirty feet, clattering like crazy. I had no idea that horse could run like that. He is headed toward the woods, and I know that is not good. That horse is about my only source of entertainment.

Darn It! Maybe I Missed Something!

After a while I find him. Sure enough, he is hung up on some persimmon sprouts. He's backing off that set of wheels like a real working horse backs off a calf, except nothing is moving. That rope is tight as a guitar string, the saddle girth is straining, and the horse is staring wall-eyed at that set of wheels and the shaking bushes, snorting all the while and tossing his head. I'm sure glad I had taught him to trust me, because after a bit I was able to calm him down and unhook him from the mess he was in.

I finished that story to make a point. I think some folks are tied to their way of doing things like that horse was tied to those wagon wheels. It seems okay in the beginning, but when it comes apart, they don't dare to look back to see what the difficulty is. They just run with it. Years later they find themselves all tangled in undergrowth that shouldn't be there. They are staring wall-eyed at something that is wrong. They don't completely understand the problem. Somehow they've become afraid to walk up on that thing and look it over. I might have missed something, but I think much of the way folks pray could be like that. Notice that I am not using absolute language here. Could it be that even our efforts in prayer have gotten off track?

While it might be surprising to some, I have thought about that. God has become so important to me. I'm just beginning to realize that He not only accepts me, He likes me. When He showed me that, it really messed me up. For years I had been convinced that I was everything He did not like. It seems to me that my life really changed when I understood that. God, Almighty, Creator of the universe, King, and Savior provided for my salvation because He likes me. He called me friend. He started talking to me in the language of a friend. "I am with you always." Now there's a reason to clean up my language. "I will never leave you." That could really affect where I might go and what I might do while I am there. "I will never forsake you." In my thinking, there is a notion there that He might have reason to forsake me, but chooses not to. I think He knows me pretty well. I really need Him to understand from time to time while I'm learning to be His friend. So, in the thought processes of a spiritually challenged redneck, prayer becomes communication with God, my friend. You can imagine how that has caused me some problems.

There are people who are truly respected in my life. Most of them are praying people. That is not a prejudiced statement, just an observation. I am a tolerant person. Tolerant does not mean that I embrace the thinking of every other human being. If I did I would really be confused. Tolerant means that I can

Darn It! Maybe I Missed Something!

live alongside anyone who believes anything, even glean some things from their lives. But if you are looking for me to respect you, you are going to need to let me know that you realize that there must be a God in this somewhere. And that trying to communicate with Him is distinctly desirable. That's just how it is. If you can't tolerate that then you should check yourself out. Why? Because people who are praying people give testimony of just talking with God in their private life. That is good. Most of them even acknowledge that God talks back. That is good. But when I overhear some of them praying, or when they pray in public, I think I've missed something.

Some of them put on the tears and wail. I'm thinking if the lights go out you are going to need to catch half of this crowd. That wailing sounds forevermore like a ghost winding up in some dark house somewhere. Not only that, but if I had a kid come whining to me like that, I wouldn't listen to him for a minute. I would really want to slap the kid, but we know that is not acceptable. Now you know by now how my mind works. I wonder if God ever wants to slap some folks. Lord, I hope not. He could slap me from here to Sunday without half trying. I wonder what would happen if those folks just talked to God? He really does like them. What if they spent more time listening for His side of the conversation? What would it be like to just be still and know that He is God? Is there some kind of crying, wailing spirit that is receiving worship without our intending to do that? Do we dare think like that? It gives me the shivers.

Then, there is another thing I've listened in on. Since I don't have much to say with any value, I listen a lot. But what about those folks who are always telling God what He said? I suppose it's possible that He has forgotten and needs to be reminded, but I'm thinking that He doesn't age quite like we do. His memory is probably okay. Some say they pray like that to remind themselves of what God says. Try having that conversation with some of your friends. It doesn't work very well. I've tried reminding people of what they said, and it did not go well at all. However, I know that God isn't like those people. He is very tolerant of me. He doesn't always agree with me and surely does not accept all my non-sensical thinking, but He likes me. Doesn't that sound nice? God likes me. Maybe I'm missing something, but why don't they just talk to God?

Just for good measure, what about all those thees and thous? What kind of English is that? Combined with all those lists, it all becomes mass confusion in my mind. How is God ever going to communicate among all that? Amazingly enough, in all His gracious understanding, He does. But as you can see, I just can't pray like that, and it causes me problems with some folks. I don't mean it to, but when some hear me pray they feel like they need to do it over because I didn't do it right.

Or they feel the need to teach me to pray like they do. Oh, man. I just want to talk to God. I'm just getting to know Him. All that other stuff really confuses me.

Not too long back someone told me that they had really prayed hard and something or the other did not happen just like they thought it should. I'm serious when I say that I thought a long time about that. I've heard it before, so it wasn't like it took me by surprise. It just makes sense to me that if I pray and God hears me, it don't make a lot of difference how hard I pray. Anyway, what does that mean? Praying hard? I know a lot of fine and upstanding folks have talked about that, but it still don't make sense. I have been discovering God as my friend. He is closer to me than my brothers, and I like them a lot. I am going to have a lot of trouble thinking that He will hold off on answering my prayers, my communication, until I reach a certain level of hardness. In Oklahoma we say something is hard when other folks would say it was difficult. Another person said that maybe God needed us to say specifically what it is we need. One guy I know went so far as to learn all the parts of the human body so he could pray for healing more effectively. That might be okay for some, but what about folks who just can't memorize all those little bones and intestines and organs? Does that leave them out? What about the Bible itself saying that we don't know what to ask for, that the Holy Spirit does that for us? I imagine He knows all that He needs to know about the specifics.

I'm having great success just talking to God. I've found out I need to be careful what I ask Him to do. He might do it just because we are friends. Some of the things I think I need from Him would not be good for me at all. I know that doesn't apply to you, but life has taught me that I do not always know what is good for me. That wagon story isn't the only true story in my life. Sometimes I think it is best for me to just ask God to lead me and guide me. A lot of the time I find that I just want to talk to Him about things that don't matter to some other folks. I even asked Him a few times if I would be forced to live in one of those mansions that the songs describe. I know. This is surprising. I would not have been surprised if He had refused to answer me. Almost immediately I sensed the assurance in my heart that it would not be necessary. For a guy who loves simple living and the great outdoors, that was a true relief, and I considered it one of God's greatest blessings.

I might be missing something, but the God that I am discovering is changing my life. I doubt that I will ever be into the moaning and crying. I know His first name is not Ohhhh. At any rate, now I have hope that I am accepted into His family. I don't feel that I will go to hell or that I have sinned away my day of grace. I am still rough. I don't fit in with a lot of religious folk, but somehow I am getting comfortable with God.

WHAT DO YOU MEAN "JESUS IS THE SWEETEST NAME I KNOW"?

I don't mean any disrespect, but that song and statement bother me. For an Oklahoma farm boy, the idea of a man that is sweet is not a good thing. It has been pounded into me from the day I could understand that *sweet* might be a term to describe girls, but it's not a part of a boy's makeup. That has been instilled in me so strong that when I hear them singing that song, I just don't want to be a part of anything like it. I know. It's probably not right, but I don't like it. I'm pretty sure my daddy don't like it either. He don't say anything, but he don't jump on that song like some other folks do. Any way you cut it, it matters to a boy of any age when his daddy don't get on board with something. There are some guys who do get into it, though. They yodel out that song, arms raised, eyes closed. I can't help but wonder: what are they really thinking? Have they really thought about that? Do they ever consider what kind of message they might be sending to the young men around them?

Now, I'm wondering about myself again. Is being sweet expected of me? Can I do it? Does God expect it of me? Maybe I'm not so accepted after all. I know people think that the Bible says that, but I haven't found it, and I've done considerable looking. I know that guy, Solomon, wrote a lot of syrupy, sweet things to women he was after—I've got some understanding of that—but Solomon turned out to be wise in some ways, but really dumb in others. Solomon wasn't so bright in the woman department. I don't feel the need to equate what he wrote with what I need to sing and feel about Jesus. Darn it! I must be missing something! I am truly sorry. I don't want to offend God or others who serve Him, but I just can't go there.

Now, I'm almost back to where I started. I almost feel like God is about to drop the hammer on me. I can't get into that kind of stuff, and it's coming close to certain that He is going to judge me. But, if I did that, it wouldn't be right. I don't feel that way, and I am not going to act like I do. (In good Oklahoma vernacular—you like that word? So do I!) I just ain't going to do it. God can change me, but I reckon He'll have to do it. It ain't in me. I told you I am a mess!

As I consider all these feelings inside me, I begin to remember all I've gone through to get this far. It wasn't that long ago that I thought that God would never give me a chance. I recall that I had already proven that God was different than I first thought. He seemed to come looking for me when I thought I had no chance with Him. It just naturally follows, at least in my thinking, that He must know me. He doesn't just know that I exist, but He knows me. I read somewhere in the Psalms—don't you just love to read those high-sounding writings?—that He remembers He is our Father. That will be a whole different chapter, but it still seems to me that I am accepted. Not so much because I am human, but because I am me. The point is, surely God knew we would hit this spot. You know, considering that He knows me and all, He's probably aware that no matter how sweet He seems to be, I'm not going to feel good about saying that and acting that way. No matter how smooth Solomon was with words, God is very likely aware that I'm not that smooth and don't want to be.

I'm going to go on in the exact same way that I got started. I began this thing knowing that I was wrong. It wasn't about the things I had done—although those were considerable and bad—it was about what I had become. One who had been created in the likeness and image of God. One who had the ability to touch other lives. One who in a negative way had done just that. That person—me—had to come to Jesus just as I was. And wonder of wonders, He changed me. The most amazing thing about walking with Him and talking with Him is that as I discover Him, I find I am becoming like Him. So I'm not quitting. I'm not proud that I am different from some other people, but I know that I am. If I just mimicked them, I would not be as I am. It could be that someday—now, I said could be—I'll feel what I feel and Jesus will become "sweet" to me. Actually, I'm kind of doubting that. But I am also aware of some place in the Bible that says that when I am faithless that He will remain faithful. I am so glad that He is full of faith. Sometimes I am bumping on empty. I suppose I could confess something or other, but that doesn't really seem honest to me. I'm not denying that others seem to have it figured out. I just don't. And I want to at least feel like I am being honest when I talk to God. Maybe I missed something. I'm pretty sure I did.

    I can hardly believe this feeling. I think He likes me. Even after all that stuff that borders on irreverence. What a God He is. He truly is like a Father. I can understand that because my own dad was a great guy. You could only push him so far. After that it seemed like the wrath of God came down on you, but then it was all over and he was just Dad again. I was always interested in fast cars, powerful pick-up trucks, and big machinery. Some folks say they have neon in their veins. I had a mix of diesel and gasoline in mine. When I was in my late teens, Dad bought a new Chevy truck with a big V-8 in it. He let me drive it anytime he wasn't using it. He always admonished me, "Be careful with it. It has more power than it needs." Well, you can guess the rest. I never could resist the feel of speed and power. I reckon I didn't try very hard.

I brought that truck back late one night and went to bed. At four thirty the next morning, Dad was standing by my bed. It seemed that he wanted me to go out to the truck with him. It wasn't a suggestion. When we got out to the truck, it became apparent that he had already made one trip. He had a big metal box filled with tools that sat in a certain position in the bed of the truck. In certain situations, like sliding around corners, taking curves almost on two wheels—you get the idea—that box would slide around. I would have to remember where to position that box before I got home. That was not devious, just self-preservation. Dad had played a big part in bringing me into this world. He let it be known that he would not be totally against taking me out. I believed him.

Anyway, the previous night I had been careless. I hadn't repositioned the box. That was dumb. This time Dad didn't seem angry. He just pointed it out and grinned that grin of his. Some of you know. The grin that says, "I know. I even understand, but don't be mistreating my truck. You might be seventeen, but that don't cut any ice with me." Well, I thought it was over, but when he returned home about dark that evening, there was more to it. That truck had developed a knock on the way home from work. I was a trained mechanic by then. We both knew that was a new and very trustworthy engine. That rod-bearing knock was an indication that the engine had been highly overstressed. I did have current knowledge that the speedometer on that truck would go all the way around, past 100 miles per hour, and wrap back around and up to ten miles per hour. We have some long, straight stretches of road in Oklahoma. He only said, "Listen to this." Then he fired it up. I nodded and with great insight and understanding said, "Why don't you take my car tomorrow? I have a friend who will let me use his shop to rebuild that engine." Again, that grin. The eyes were glinting behind it. He knew that rebuild job would not cost him one penny. I worked. I had money. I had made a grave mistake. I would make restitution. No grinding on the existing crankshaft. No easy fixes. That engine would be better than new. And it was.

God, our Father is somewhat like that. He brings things to my attention. He acknowledges my increasing stature and maturity by just calling my attention to it and then waiting to see if I will do the right thing. I know it is just me, but sometimes I think I can sense a grin on His face, a bit like my natural dad. Knowing these things has helped me to recognize other parts of the relationship between God and me. Sometimes I feel like He is far from me. When that happens I think about my dad and me. There were many times when I was growing up that Dad and I were far apart. I just didn't feel close. Invariably those times were my own fault. Maybe I did something that I knew my dad disapproved of. I didn't want to tell him the truth of it. Many times I knew that if I told him then I would have to stop doing that thing. It was just the natural way that it worked. No matter what, whenever I was willing to face my own problem, and most of the time get his help repairing the damage, my dad would be right there ready and willing. Looking back, it seems that he had never moved. I had. Surprisingly enough, God is like that. He doesn't change much. At any time that I am ready to face my issues, He is right there, ready to walk on with me while He and I repair the damages. He allows me to correct myself. He says He doesn't change at all. I believe Him. I've tried to change Him to match my theology. It never works. That is very difficult for a hard head like me.

No matter where my thinking and my living take me, I am still struck by a fact that humbles me. He knows all about what I've done and what I've not done, and He still likes me. I even think He likes the way I look. Or He is amused by it. I'm still not sure which.

He likes the way I am. I have this sure knowledge deep in my soul that He isn't offended because I'm a man. I'm talking about a real man here. I feel His approval. He must have planned for me to be different than women. I don't think I'm missing anything here.

OH BOY! THIS HEAVEN THING IS A WHOLE DIFFERENT DEAL

I keep hearing things about heaven that make me wonder if I want to go. I know I am not supposed to think that way. I've tried to like what I hear and what the songs say. I've also tried it my way. You know, I think a lot of men do this. I just try to push it away and not think about it, but the next thing I know, here it comes again. I'm trying to be respectful and reverent—in case you didn't notice, that don't come easy for me—but I just don't like the thought of kneeling around a throne somewhere for eternity. All those mansions, shining and polished, wearing white robes, or wearing nothing, having some monstrosity of a crown on my head—sorry about the description—all those things really bother me. Come on now, do you want to spend whatever eternity is trying not to laugh? Every time you take a break from the harp and the kneeling, there are all those people wearing a crown and nothing else. If you're really honest, you know that you will want a break, and you will be tempted to laugh.

That is just a small part of what I've thought about these things. Most of the rest of my thinking is best not put in print. However, it truly became apparent to me that I should go to the Bible, just open myself up to the Holy Spirit, and see what He would show me. What a revelation it was when I realized that some of the things in the Bible are simpler than we make them. Just be bold enough to think about these things. Be bold enough! If you were John on the Isle of Patmos and all these visions began to come to you; if God began to show you some things that were a couple of thousand years away, how would you explain all the technology that would develop in between? How would you describe the warfare that would be waged? All you could do would be to try to say it in a way that would help others of your day to understand in a limited way. I even think that you and I might expect some common sense to intervene as we tried to understand. But that's just me, and maybe I'm missing something. No matter what I am missing, these were some of the problems faced by the writers of the early New Testament Scripture.

I think of the beauty of possibility of the passage in the Gospel of John. Jesus was talking to a group of men who would be emotionally devastated by His death. He was going away, and He needed them to understand. If He couldn't get them to grasp it now, at least He could leave them something to help them when He was gone. He told them He was going away to prepare a place for them. He wanted them to experience as much of Him and His interaction with His Father as possible. Using present tense in His speaking, He said they could be with Him. He and His Father would take up residence—dwell—with them. Through the work of His death and resurrection, He would accomplish that which would be a great blessing for all mankind. The door would be open for you and me to live and be involved in the life of God.

When that is coupled with a small change in our thinking about the book of Revelation, everything begins to change. Wouldn't it be reasonable to allow John to tell us what the Revelation was about? When he wrote that it was the Revelation of Jesus Christ, doesn't it make sense just to allow it to be that? How did we ever get to the idea that it was anything else? Maybe the theologians have the answer to that, but neither Jesus nor John were theologians! As the scope of this whole thing begins to dawn on me, I am more and more interested in following Jesus and discovering Him. In the first few chapters, I get this amazing picture of Jesus Christ and am humbled by the idea of Him always being present among the churches. Much of what I have heard about these chapters seems to focus on what is wrong with those churches. I readily admit that does concern me. But what I am most impressed with is the fact that He is still moving among them and recognizing them as His own. Now these are just my ideas, my thoughts, but wouldn't it be good for all of us who are involved in the church to realize that His focus isn't really on all the problems that we have? Certainly He observes those problems and points them out. Yet the focus seems to be somewhat different. It appears that all we need to repair the damage is to rejoin Him in our journey into eternity as the kingdom of God. There is a real reason for thinking like this. I will make an attempt to illustrate what I'm thinking.

One of the men who greatly impacted my life through Bible teaching lived for several years in New York City. He became friends with a man whose job was with one of the large zoos in the area. Every morning this man fed and cared for the reptiles. Personally, I am very glad that was his job and not mine. Being an Oklahoma boy, I am more likely to shoot a snake than to feed it. However, my friend got a call one morning. This man asked him to come down to the zoo. He had received a new snake the day before and thought it could be of interest. While the men stood outside the snake area, another worker released a small bird into the cage. As soon as the snake saw the bird, it began to focus its attention on the bird. The snake stared and followed every movement of that bird. After a short time, the bird began to look at the snake. Soon the snake and the bird locked gazes. An amazing sequence of events followed. The bird had every opportunity to continue to fly out of the snake's reach, but when their gazes locked, the bird landed and began to slowly hop lower and lower. The bird was completely fascinated by the snake. After a short time, the bird was within striking range of the snake. The bird became lunch.

As my friend related this story, I realized that sin is like that snake. If I focus on sin, I become very vulnerable to its dangers. I have every opportunity to walk with Jesus. He will be faithful to point out the things that would keep me from the fullness of His life. We can work together and completely leave behind those issues that He has called to my attention. On the other hand, if I get all caught up in the things that have been mentioned as wrong, I will fall into their trap every time. I'm reasonably sure that John was just pointing out that although some things were off in those churches, Jesus was still moving among them. If we rejoin Him, we will find Him ready and willing to help us move up in the kingdom. Kind of like He said to John, "Come up here!" There must be a place where we can live in Him; a place that takes us above all the focus on sin. It could be that is what Paul was talking about when he wrote about being seated in heavenly places. Or if you insist, I guess Paul could have been talking about a sitting room in a mansion that sits close to some throne. I doubt it. I sincerely doubt it.

From the place John was called to there was a view that gets more amazing—I know I keep using that word, but it's truly how I feel—as I go along. The view boggles my mind. John saw things from beginning to end. How easy it would be to get embroiled in the controversy that surrounds all the doctrinal opinions these things have bred. I am convinced that all those opinions were put forth with the best of intentions, but some of them sure confuse me. For my purposes, which include and mostly consist of trying to know and please God, why can't we just accept that Jesus was revealing Himself and His work among men to John?

Something wonderful happens to my faith when I look at these chapters in this way. If I have questions regarding Abraham and his walk with God, Jesus Christ is well able to help me know the answers. If I am wondering about things to come, Jesus is well able to help me see that picture of people of every nation, tribe, and tongue worshiping. Somehow I know this is so important to our Father. The wonder, the mystery of God, and His plan remains intact, unexplainable to me. Yet I am struck by humility as I see that I have some small part in the forming of that multitude of worshipers. The picture of present time builds as my awe of God increases. I realize that I have a "crown" of authority in the world of God. I share in the coronation of Jesus Christ. As I mature I will become more and more adept in making my life a life of worship. In a very real sense I cast, lay, my authority at His feet. I will make no moves without His first moving. I will assume no authority that He isn't urging me to take. I am becoming mature in His kingdom, His house.

Could this possibly be what Paul was saying when he talked about things being by faith? Is it plausible to think that simple explanations only serve to cause people to bow in His presence? I could be missing something, but for me this is a workable solution to the confusion that drove me away from God.

WOW! GOD UNDERSTANDS REDNECK ENGLISH!

From the very beginning, my own irreverence scared me and surprised me. Deep inside there was, and still is, a part of me that wanted to be reverent, respectful, and full of worship before God. I know now that the irreverence was normal, at least for me. But thankfully, so is my desire to develop reverence and respect, as well as to learn to live in a worshipful manner. All of us were created with that deep desire. In each of us is an inner knowledge that God is fully worthy of worship, adoration, and praise. While I will never be able to completely express those feelings I have toward Him, I can in simple expression, say, "He is God!" Some insist that *God* is a generic term. Not for me. It is simply an all-encompassing term in which I try to address all that He is.

However, there was always this conflict inside of me. If I had been born back when King James was funding the Bible translation, maybe I would have felt a lot different. Unfortunately for me, I wasn't born in that timeframe. That being the case, some of the things coming from the mouths of God's people caused me no small amount of trouble. When I say I grew up "redneck," there is no insult in that for my family or any others who grew up the same way. Redneck, in those days, was a quite different thing. It was a reference to men—some women as well—who spent time outside working for an honest day's wages. They did not grow hair—the men, anyway—down past their collars. They worked under a hot, Southern sun. Their necks were red, burned in the hot Oklahoma sun. Their politics would never be considered 'red.' In those days this was a common term for socialist views.

Throughout the South the vernacular was colorful, incorrect by the standards of most teachers, and thoroughly recognizable as Southern. The dialect varied from region to region, but all through that area many were marked by their farmers' tan, their definite and often unpopular opinions, and the idioms of language. In my early years I wasn't aware that I talked differently from other people. I heard accents now and then, but these were readily identified as belonging to immigrants or other foreigners. Foreigners were defined as anyone who moved in from the north or the east. Our world was small. Our worldview was contained completely in books on shelves. Whether it was the Ozark Mountains, Cookson Hills, Smokey Mountains, or the Big Thicket country, the language was spoken and was understandable on a broad scale.

That does not seem to be the case in church. I know men who have the finest of Arkansas/Oklahoma drawls as smooth as honey. Yet when these men start talking about God, they talk a different language entirely. Their speaking becomes laced with thees and thous. They talk about "reins of the bowels" being "loosed." Now, we know about bowels and their loosing. Anywhere that poke greens is a celebrated food folks will know about loose bowels. Again, Oklahoma folks should be proud of the way I said that. We can talk about loose bowels when folks don't know about the drizzlin's or the trots. Those things are a whole different level. But, how do you do that in King Jimmy English? At least, how is it accomplished if you are interested in keeping all us young men in the audience from busting a gut laughing? I know! It's bursting! Believe me, busting is a lot bigger thing! Have you ever seen the fierce look that crosses the faces of all the dads in the audience when young men are snorting and coughing, trying not to laugh out loud? I've always thought that was what it looked like when you wanted to laugh too. Those dads just learned to show it in a different way. They are having those mental images too. Think of the visuals! No, don't! Then you would wrestle with all this irreverence that I wrestle with. Except for one thing. Here in Oklahoma, we wrassle. That, too, is a whole different level of activity. I assume it is very easy for a normal, cultured person to have acceptable mental images while the preaching is going on. For me, it just ain't that easy. When the stories of the Bible are told with such enthusiasm, such passion as they are in rural Oklahoma, there are some words that paint pictures that a young man has great difficulty ignoring. I'm not suggesting that anyone should cultivate these, but some of those pictures are still fresh in my mind.

Remember the king who was throwing a party? I believe his name was Belshazzar. Now, I don't blame anyone for what happened. Newer versions have toned it down some. When a hand just appeared and began writing on the wall, King James English suggests a bad case of the trots. For a rough young man, that is funny. I snorted and coughed for quite some time over that one. Matter of fact, several guys on that row of seats were taken by some snorting, coughing bug about that time.

My cousin and I had a ball learning how to say, "God!" with three syllables. Since my cousin lived in the city he often visited us. On the farm we milked cows twice every day. That was prime time for us to practice all kinds of things that would possibly be important to our lives. You just never know when it will be necessary to be able to say, "Go-aw-od!" in a proper manner. I guess my mother didn't see it that way. We were practicing away, not aware that anyone was listening, when she descended on me like an avenging angel or something. I had just stepped away from the cow and was carrying a bucket of milk when she collared me. Her question was honest. "Did you know that you are taking God's name in vain?" Of course I did not know. But I made the mistake of snickering when I acknowledged my ignorance. It seems that she always thought it good to make an example of me when my less-disciplined cousins were present. I became a life illustration of the reason for practicing in silence or in the privacy of the deep woods.

To my amazement I found that God had a sense of humor. He didn't quit talking to me. I still sensed His presence when I communicated with Him. My Oklahoma dialect didn't seem to bother Him at all. In the midst of all my irreverence, and at times my disrespect, He continued to fellowship with me. Sometimes I even think He is in conversation with me. I get this sense of His voice inside of me. This could be what Paul called perceived. Just an inner sense that God is talking. Maybe I'm missing something, but I think He is talking in redneck English. Here is why I think so.

There came a time in my life when I wanted so badly to know Him, to hear Him, to really communicate. I began to pray that way. "God, I just want to know you, to understand your voice." Directly into my spirit, I could swear I heard, "Shut up!" Now, I know that is not socially correct. It could be considered verbally abusive, which is one of the dumbest things I've ever heard. But there it was. A still, small voice speaking inside me.

I knew immediately why He said that. He knew I would understand. He was giving me a basic principle that would always apply to our communication. Those things that He would say would always be more important than my talking. If I would listen, He would speak. From that time on I have found myself listening to God. He really has some special things to say. He is full of fun and laughter. When He is serious, I know it full well. If I agree not to gossip about our conversation, He will talk to me about people. If I will use the information properly, He will show me how to help people. He is a great encourager, a loving friend, and a powerful advocate.

This kind of thinking might be very uncomfortable for some people. It is not in the least uncomfortable to God. If you are Chinese, He speaks Chinese. If you are of the most remote tribal extraction, He will communicate any way that is necessary to be your Lord and Savior.

Another communication is branded into my memory. This came at a time when I was deeply aware of God's call on my life. Because of my restricted spiritual experience, I thought that responding to the call would look a certain way. In my limited experience, many of those who were called fit a definite mold. Even though I now know it is not true, at the time I categorized them all as less than real men. My response to God was heartfelt. "God, I don't want to be like them." His response was immediate and curt. "I don't want you to be like them either."

So many things can be compressed into one sentence when God is speaking. I knew right off the bat that God wasn't speaking in judgment or criticism. He was teaching me in a very concise way. He wanted the real me to respond to His will and call. His attitude toward others was reflected in Jesus's response to Peter. His approval or disapproval of those other men was not my business. My business was to do His will and work with His flock. I have never forgotten the message of that one sentence. What other men do to follow Jesus is between God and themselves. I will not be like them if I am myself.

Slowly I began to understand some things about God. Not only does He speak to me in English, but also in vernacular that is specific to my understanding. I don't know how that affects you, but this whole line of thinking greatly humbles me. How can God do that? In all this I get just a hint of His magnificence, His all-knowing capability. He uses all that He is to communicate with me. Here I am, a country boy from Oklahoma, and almighty God is willing to communicate with me. The thundering, awful voice that I had been struggling to hear is not the way He works with me. He works with perceptions, impressions, ways that will not strike me with fear and make me hesitant to open up to Him.

It's very possible that I am mistaken in this, but isn't that really what happened when Moses told the Israeli people to gather at the foot of the mountain? I'm thinking that when all that thundering and lightning began…well, they just naturally wanted to get out of there. They were possibly a bit uncomfortable about all that. I can see myself telling Moses, "You go up there if you want to! I'm not going! And if you can make anything out of all that, I'll do whatever God says."

Once again, I know by now that I have a quirk or two. Probably a little bent and twisted in my thinking. I don't think it is my "much learning" that has made me that way. However, it just could be my thinking. Especially since I'm not very careful where my thinking goes. I said that because I have been curious about something for a long time. What if people really get what they ask for from God? I mean those people who are always yowling and moaning and asking without a lot of thinking. Now, this is the kind of scenario that is in my mind. It's about dark outside. No one has turned on any lights because they are praying at God. As far as they know, no one is anywhere around. "God, touch me!" What if He did that? Don't tell me you can't get a visual on that! Or "God, show me your face!" Oh man! I can see that one. They open their eyes and there is the face of God about an inch from theirs. Anyone listening in on that one would hear the sounds of revival in that room for certain!

I remember a very honest woman from my early years. She cleaned the church in the evenings after her husband came home from work. Pastor would leave a light on in the entryway so she could see to get around while she was finding lights and cleaning supplies. One evening she opened the door and the light was not on. About that time she heard the pastor praying in the office behind the platform. His prayer went something like this. "Oh, God. Move in this church."

She immediately responded, straight from her heart. "God, if you are in here, you be real still until I find the lights." I really am convinced that most of us would feel like that.

MAYBE HE AIN'T A SCHIZO!

Sometimes I really worry about me. It seems that every little thing I am not allowed to do, I do! I'm almost convinced that God is schizophrenic! That worries me on more than one level. The first, and no doubt the most serious, is that I think that way about God. He is the Master of the universe. One word from Him and I am history. But I keep hearing things that cause my mind to go off on one of its musing sessions. Some things I hear make me think that God is just waiting for me to mess up and then He will smash me. I don't have any difficulty believing that He can do that. I read all those stories in the Old Testament. I am convinced He can do anything He decides to do.

As I think about this, I'm reminded of the way some people try to train a puppy. Every time that pup messes up they call him to them. "Here, puppy. Come over here." The pup doesn't know they are holding a rolled-up newspaper behind them. At least, the first time he doesn't know. Then after all that friendliness they smack him with the paper and say, "Bad dog!" Then they throw him outside. Darn it! I'm probably missing something, but it just seems like God is like that. At least, to some folks He is like that.

Then, almost in the same message, He is talked about as a loving Father. That is surely confusing to me. Is God really like me? Is He moody? Does He wake up some mornings and not feel well? It sure seems to me that He has at least two personalities. The problem for me is very simple. I'm a lot like that puppy. I need to know what to do. I want to please God, but I have these things in my life that need changing. Is God going to give me a chance, or not? Are we going to be going along, everything seems to be just fine, then, *bam!* He whacks me? Removes Himself from me? Maybe tosses me out? If that is the way of it, I need to know. One thing I know for sure—I have proved this—I will mess up! Badly and often! However, another thing I know is that I don't want to. I really want to know God and please Him.

Once again, I go on a search through the Bible. I've gotten the idea that for some folks the Bible is a book that records God's hand of judgment on people. As I've read it, though, I've found it to be something quite different. This book, this Bible, has become a source of knowledge and comfort to me. In it I can find answers that help me to control these musings of my mind. It seems as if this book actually begins to channel my thoughts into right directions, right thinking. Instead of this book consisting of judgment, I think it is a record. In this record I find the many things God will do to save His greatest creative accomplishment—man. I am constantly astounded at the lengths to which He will go to touch and redeem one life. He gave Philip a real air ride just to touch one eunuch.

With this and many more stories in mind, I can adjust my thinking to a more acceptable mode. I realize that the authors of the Bible also went to great lengths to write the things they saw and heard in a way that will be understood. I know I am missing some things, but now I can apply the same reasoning to more modern commentary and even some preachers. When I hear or read about the trinity, I'm not quite so confused. I realize that men are making their best effort to wrap words around the amazing and profound things they see in the Word of God. In as simple a way as possible, they are trying to explain the fact of a God who is many faceted, but with decided personal traits. True amazement begins to dawn in my thinking. I realize that all the languages of the world are not vast enough to encompass and explain God. At the same time He is bringing me along, causing me to grow and mature, recognizing my weaknesses, and refusing to be dismayed by them, He could be overseeing the final turns of the wheel of judgment in another part of the world, and it is all a part of who He is and the job He has undertaken in the salvation of mankind.

This kind of thinking brings a lot of relief into my heart. I figure if I have any chance at all, I must know who my enemy is. If for one moment I think God is my enemy, I am finished. I have developed a healthy respect, awe, and admiration for who He is. If His hand is against me, I give up now. But I read about Him. Everything good comes from Him. If there is anything perfect—I know! That doesn't include me! That is not my category, perfect!—it is from Him. Once He sets out on a path, there is not even a shadow of turning back. Why does this help me so much? He started on a road with me. He came looking for me when I didn't think I could ever know Him. I know I might be missing something, but what I do know is that He has changed my life. He has also walked with me through all the irreverent musings that I have to deal with. He has truly begun a good work in me. As I read His Word, I am convinced He will stay with it. He is not going to give up on me. That is not in His nature.

Seems to me that all this keeps going back to the Bible. At first I read it because I thought I had to read it. It was some kind of qualification I had to meet. I had to read every day, pray every day, and even do some memorization—and that is *really* difficult for me! As I worked hard to meet all the qualifications, the whole thing changed. Now I want to read the Bible. It has become a book of discovery for me. Even in the genealogy I get a chuckle or two. How would you like to be named Peleg? For a boy in Oklahoma, that would be an exercise in martial arts! Speaking of chuckles, what about the donkey—(See? I am getting better! I didn't write "ass," even though King James gives me the right! Oops! Guess I did!)—talking to the prophet? I just might have met some prophets that could benefit from such an experience.

Writing all this makes me feel sorry for the early Christians. They didn't have a Bible on their nightstand. Or even in their home. I cannot imagine living righteously with only one weekly message to go by. Many of them couldn't read, but even if they had been able to, there were very few copies of the Old Testament available. The New Testament was still being written. At best they had only the occasional letter, which was read to them. Yet they knew God. He made Himself real to them. He impressed His will and His ways upon them. He changed their lives, saved their families, impacted their cities, and caused them to call upon Him in prayer. What a God we serve.

One of the most amazing parts of this is that He has brought my thinking into line with His personality. He did not get angry about my frustration, my doubt. He did not give up on me when my musings went beyond the accepted parameters. He allowed me to sense His presence all the way through it. And at this point, I know I am missing some things. That is exciting to me. God has stayed with me this far. I know that we have many more things to ponder. I will make more mistakes that He will help me correct. Much more importantly, there are many more facets of His personality to be discovered. Just this past week, a friend of mine uncovered another facet that I had never thought of. His comment was this: "Our God is a drama God!" The statement stopped me in midsentence. How much of life could that explain? How many times was the drama in my life actually planned by Him? Much more challenging, even a bit scary, how many more dramatic scenes does He have planned for me? Dramatic deliverances? Dramatic healings? Dramatic conversions? Hey, God, let's get on with it. I can't wait to see what You do. Some of it I think I could do without, but You, God, in all Your wisdom have determined that this drama is a part of my inclusion in the great, sweeping saga of Your dealings with Your people. I bow to Your decision.

God's personality is not split. He is simply the most complex being we will ever have dealings with. What a wonder. He invites us to know Him. I know I am missing some things, but I am trying hard to discover Him—in the power of His resurrection; in the fellowship of His suffering; and, yes, even that, being conformed to His death.

I STILL AIN'T LIKING THE IDEA OF FIGHTING A DEVIL I CAN'T SEE!

All of my life, I've been a dedicated reader. From the time I learned to read, I've always read anything that's available at the time. These days, it seems like everywhere I turn there is a book on spiritual warfare. In this arena I truly think I might be missing something. As I read these books, I can't help but remember all the scriptures I've read in the Bible over the years and much of what is written about spiritual warfare didn't surface in my Bible studies. Darn it! Maybe I'm missing something! Again!

I'm guessing here, but as I read some of this spiritual warfare writing, it seems there is a basic trait of human nature that some might be overlooking. Very early in my pursuit of understanding it seemed that something was just a little bit off. When that happens the problem is more basic than we think. I remember an Appaloosa gelding I had when I was younger. I know that many horse trainers would argue with this, but I simply could not work cattle with that horse. He was high strung, as we would say in Oklahoma. If a leaf fluttered beside him, he was off and running. That horse looked for reasons to run. The few times I tried to work cattle with him, he caused several mini stampedes. If a steer would run, off he would go after it, from zero to thirty-five miles an hour in a few jumps. No matter if a simple trot would do, he was off and running. The bad part was he would bite that steer on the rump to make it go faster. Since I had trained him to a hackamore, I had no bit to pull him back. If I stayed on, okay. If I didn't he was still chasing that steer. It did not make for a good roundup. Some would say he needed training, but in reality there was a basic need in that horse. He needed to run. He loved to chase anything. If I "broke" him of it, then I would have changed his nature. I didn't do that. I wanted him to be what he was made to be.

As human beings, made in the image of God, we need to take time to look at consistent traits, ways of behavior that are deep in our being. Much of this spiritual warfare writing seems to overlook one of those traits. We have a basic need to play a part in our own salvation, our rescue from the powers of darkness—look at that! Powers of darkness! I've learned some more church-speak! Having a part in our salvation is good. I am certain our Lord and Savior does not want to "break" us of that. The apostle Paul picked up on that in his writings. When he says that we are workers together with Him I get a "feel good feeling" all over me. I get this picture in my mind of the Holy Spirit alongside Paul, alongside me, doing things that have made a difference in our lives and the lives of those to whom we minister. Since we were made like that, we can be certain that our Father does not want to change that part of our nature. If we can identify things that are basic to humanity, then our list of things needing change will shorten considerably.

In my thinking, we need to allow the great truths of the Bible to guide us as we decide what it is that God wants us to be involved with. Personally, I have a crazy side to my nature. That has been mellowed out some with age, but it is still there. I will tackle almost anything. When I was a kid we had an old chicken house out behind the barn. Since the coyotes liked the chickens more than we did, the chicken house was used for raising calves. There was a corner inside the chicken house where we could close in a calf and give him the necessary shots and perform other unmentionable "medical" procedures—goodness! How time tempers the language! My dad and I decided one of our calves needed a shot. The calf would have weighed out at 500 pounds or more. At the time I would have weighed 175 pounds or less. Dad told me, "Don't get in front of him if he decides to make a break for it!" Well, like I said, I have a crazy streak in me. Even while Dad was saying it, I knew I was stronger than he thought, and that calf was not getting by me.

Everything went reasonably well up to the time Dad hit the calf with the needle. We had him all pressed up against the wall. The calf had settled down. His resistance seemed to be at an end. Dad and I were leaning our weight into him, holding him into a corner and against the wall. The calf's head was pointed toward the door, but we had him where we needed him. Then Dad hit him with the needle. The calf wasn't finished with his resisting. With that big silver needle waving around on his hip, his tail twisting as only a half Holstein, half Hereford can, he headed for the door of the chicken house. I knew I could stop him! I grabbed his head, thinking I would throw him like they do in the rodeo. In the grabbing, I made one big mistake. I got in front of his head instead of alongside it. Now, not only is the calf heading toward the door, I am too, backward, bent double over his head. The needle fell out, safe and sound. I needed someone or something to help me turn him loose. The narrow doorway accomplished that. The threshold was about eight inches off the ground. My feet hit the threshold, my butt hit the ground outside, and the calf ran right over me on his way back out to the pasture. Another basic human trait is that we generally heal up fairly quickly when we are young. I took full advantage of that while growing up. However, I am very likely forever damaged. My dad actually had to recover from his laughing before he could check the needle to see if he got all the medication into the hip of the calf. After that, he did ask me if I was all right.

Now, if I thought there was anything to be gained by going after the devil, I reckon I would do that. However, if I were to embrace that line of thinking, I would have to ignore a lot of Bible record. Darn it! Maybe I'm missing something, but I think Jesus has that covered. As I have read and studied my mind has gone through a lot. I like to get into the Word of God and live it in my mind. On the screen of my mind it gets very adventuresome at times. At times it really seemed like the devil was going to win. Over and over I have been awestruck at the sheer manhood of Jesus. None of the soft preacher for this one. Some of the suggestions of the entire story are astounding. Jesus could have called legions of angels to help him, but He didn't. What a man! But think of it from the angels' point of view. This man Jesus was the only begotten son of God, Himself. From my rather extreme point of view, He was representative of God's greatest effort, experiment, if you would allow me to call it that. The angels must have been straining to get involved in the battle. How often they must have thought their intervention was necessary. As the whip whistled through the air and connected with a sodden thump on His naked back, how their muscles must have swelled and strained. "Just say the word, Jesus!" "One hint of permission and we will take out the whole power of darkness!" How they must have waited, hardly breathing, to see His body begin to twitch, breathe, and respond to the Holy Spirit.

He won the battle! Now, I don't think I am missing anything there. My God is not a prisoner in His heaven, waiting for me to yell enough, bind enough, and go through enough to break Him free. The devil's angels are incapable of interfering with whatever my God has determined to do. Is it possible that if I understand more fully the intention of God I can truly wage a mighty warfare? I am personally appalled by what is being suggested as prayer. Isn't prayer in all its forms to be simply communication with God? Aren't we encouraged in Scripture to come to Him in all the facets of His person?

I guess the part that bothers me the most is that some are talking to the devil and calling it a form of prayer. Thank you, but no thank you. I'll take my chances talking to God. He truly wants to talk to us. He wants us to enforce and reinforce all the victory that Jesus accomplished as He submitted to crucifixion and responded to resurrection. Our basic need to be involved can be perfectly satisfied by judging the lies the enemy has caused us to believe and act on. As we replace those lies with the truth of God, then the enemy will be defeated in our personal lives. What a way to live! I can relax into serving God. I can be spiritually natural and naturally spiritual. I can live out the victory that Christ has already won.

I learned a lot while being run over by that steer. From that day to now I am very respectful of how my body is placed in relation to the head of any bovine beast. Much of life is like that. When we challenge the powers of darkness in an unnatural way, we find ourselves being trampled. In my simple Oklahoma way of thinking, I can hear the warning of the Holy Spirit. "Quit picking fights with the powers of darkness! Don't get all wrapped up in wrassling—(yes, I remember it's wrestling!)—with a defeated foe!"

There are some simple Bible study techniques I have found through the years. One is so simple that I would have missed it if some of the scholars did not keep reminding me. It is this. Allow the writers to illustrate without making doctrine out of the illustration. With that in mind, consider the life of the apostle Paul. He spent many of his writing years in very close proximity to Roman soldiers. Guarded by a soldier much of the time and actually chained to a soldier some of the time. How natural it would be for his illustrations to come to him as he wrote with a soldier in his line of sight, hearing the clank of sword against armor. As he watches the armor bearer pull the laces of the girdle tight around the groin of the soldier. How easy to write, "The weapons of our warfare are not carnal, but they are mighty through God. Put on the whole armor of God."

While never intended to be doctrinal, these graphic illustrations make wonderful word pictures in our mind. They cause us to rise up in our thinking. They propel us into a determined posture as we pull the lies of the enemy out of our lives and insert the truth of a Savior who paid more than enough for our salvation. We know without any doubt that God's supernatural power rests upon our natural person to help us and empower us to become all that we can be in Him. All the struggles that we face demand that we be good soldiers, not picking fights against the enemy, but living in celebration of the war that has been won. To us our Father has entrusted the preparing and keeping of the bride of His Son. She will truly be a glorious bride, without spot or wrinkle. Maybe I'm missing something, but this is a great life I live in the shadow of His triumph over darkness.

IS HEARING GOD AS EASY AS THEY SAY?

It's a big day at our house. I've only been out of the U.S. Navy for a few months. Since I left the world of big guns, bonca boats, and helicopters, I was looking for a place to just live for a while. In the Ozark Mountains I had found what I needed for now. While climbing those rugged mountains and then sitting for long hours at the top, I found a place of healing for my troubled soul. On this morning three of my cousins from Oklahoma will be joining me for the opening day of deer season. We will take our four-wheel-drive pick-up truck and drive an old logging road five or six miles back into those beautiful mountains. All of us have hunted most of our lives. There is an understanding among us. We are hunters, no doubt about it. However, we are not there for the kill, but for the relationships, for the sheer joy of just being out in such beautiful countryside.

At this time in our lives, only one of us had come to know God. His life had changed. None of us had any doubt about it. This man was a few years older than the other cousins. He had been a hero, a role model to all of us. In the tried and true tradition of the hills of Oklahoma and the mountains of Arkansas, this man was known as a fighter. Not just that, but he would stand in protection for any member of the family. We all were very aware that he had more than just an encounter with God. That encounter had changed his life. He would tell you that God had saved his marriage, changed his family. More than that, this change had continued for more than six years. Six years! All that time his family was declaring the obvious—at least it seemed obvious to us. "He's not going to make it!" "It won't last!" We just knew how it was in our neck of the woods. If a man got in trouble with his wife—she was going to leave, take the kids—he would often get religion. By the time everything settled down, he would be right back into the old ways, which is a nice way to say, "He is right back in trouble!"

But he was already six years into this change. Most of us had stopped trying to prophesy his downfall and were watching his life. By now we felt a kind of awe about this change. We had not heard about any fighting outside bars—at least, not with him involved. We had been around him some; however, we were very careful about that. Religion can rub off on you. Nobody had heard him cuss. Yes, I know some think it is cursing, but some of the cussing I've heard has different tones than that. It is not quite so cultured as cursing and has a much greater vocabulary range. I'm just observing. Anyhow, we knew there was a genuine change. Without any talk among us, all of the other three knew what we would do. If he started in about religion, we would grab a gun and make a break for the woods.

But I had a problem. I had been in these woods long enough then for them to work some of their magic on me. As I spent hours on end looking at and experiencing God's creation a greater and greater hunger was building inside me. I truly wanted to know Him, but I was very uncertain how to proceed. My situation reminded me of a deer I had been watching for several mornings. He was a nice buck. The season hadn't yet opened, so all I could do is watch. You understand, I'm sure. By now the game and fish people had started confiscating pickup trucks and guns, as well as arresting hunters if they broke the law. No one in their right mind would risk their guns and certainly not their pickup truck. So this buck was as safe as he could be. I was only watching; the guns were safely in the truck. I never was one to resist temptation while hunting. I knew it was best to leave the gun.

The weather was unusually cold for November in Arkansas. All the ponds were frozen over, leaving a small open area in the middle. This deer really wanted that water. As he looked at it, you could almost see the thirst building up in him. He stepped very gingerly out on that pond, and about the third step one leg slid out from under him. He dashed back to shore, legs slipping and sliding. Then there he was, looking at that open water again. There were running streams within two or three hundred yards, but that buck wanted the water in that pond. One time he almost made it to the open water. I think he heard the ice crack, because something startled him. He slipped, slid, and flailed for the longest time. Finally he settled down and very slowly walked back to shore. Even then he looked back over his shoulder several times as he walked away toward one of the streams.

I could identify with that buck. I have some questions about God. I feel like I am looking at something that I want very much, but I have all this bad behavior to deal with. I'm not doing so much of that now, but it is in my past. In truth it seems to live in me every time I think about God. I've been convinced that I will end up in hell. I don't think about that much. My mind is full of sinful living. I remember the messages I've heard about sinning away my day of grace. To compound my sinful life, I resisted those altar calls. I still don't want to walk down an aisle somewhere and have a bunch of howling women gather around me and cry. I think I even recognize *that* attitude as sin, but I just can't find it in myself to do it. That is why I thought I couldn't just ask God. I really think He don't want to talk to me. There are some things I just can't seem to do. I'm not having any luck getting myself to clean up my life so I can present myself before Him. I don't have any memories that make me think God will accept me as I am. So why walk that aisle when I'm not going to be accepted anyway? Besides that, I have questions. But I'm not qualified to question. So, like the buck wanting water, I'm finding the way to God very slippery.

I have a pastor who is very interesting to listen to. He treats me like a human being. I don't go very often, but he comes by my house sometimes. I'm very careful to have somewhere to go or something to do when he drops by. But I do go to church occasionally. It's usually when my two-year-old daughter is crying because she wants to go to Sunday school. My wife won't take her unless I go. Seems like a conspiracy to me. Anyway, I've seen the pastor when someone asks him a question that might be controversial. Why does he get so mad? I think that they really want to know. I'm listening because I want to know too. Through this I have become a listener instead of a questioner. I don't want any attention drawn to me. The things I've done and the way I've lived, sometimes out of necessity, are not things I want drawn out in public. On top of that, I don't respond too well when someone turns red and gets loud when talking to me. Particularly if I have asked a simple question.

All this has worked together to keep me listening while my cousin talks in deer camp, and he is a talker. When his mouth is in gear, it is a pure wonder the volume of words he can generate. I don't remember all that he said. I do remember that he wasn't wasting this opportunity to talk about God among this group of heathens. Somewhere in it all he made a statement that got inside me. "There is no middle ground. You either serve God or the devil." He got right inside me with that one. I left the campfire, crawled into my sleeping bag, and made every effort to make them all think I was sleeping. In truth, I don't think I slept thirty minutes. I was struggling with that statement. I had grown up in a world of absolute loyalties, misplaced or not. I knew about taking sides and living it out for better or worse. I am mortified at the reality of how I had lived, how I had talked, the side I had been taking.

Around four thirty the next morning, I was sitting beside an old log, waiting for the first light of day to dawn. All the deer in the woods were safe that morning. I was talking to God. I was telling Him that I did not know what I was doing. I had never considered whether or not the devil was being served. I was still convinced that I was unacceptable to God. I wasn't trying to get Him to treat me the same way He treated other people. I was just talking to Him about my regrets. I thought I was just living life and having fun. I remember one statement as if it were yesterday. "God, I am going to serve you. I know I am not acceptable. I have done most of the things that will separate me from you. Even if I split hell wide open, I will do my best to serve you. I am on your side, God."

Being a Vietnam-era veteran, a tried and true member of the Tonkin Gulf Yacht Club, I do have a tight hold on my emotions. I have learned to use my emotions and not allow them to use me. I can tell you that I felt nothing on that morning. My cousin had talked some about God talking to him. As near as I can tell, He still isn't talking to me. If He were to talk to me in an audible voice, I would very likely still be beside that log at this moment, ducking down, blending with the foliage, and waiting for Him to make a move I could identify. I was still very dumb about God.

But, my life began to change. I wasn't wanting to go back to the old sinful way of life and living. I lost at least 75 percent of my vocabulary. Over time the foul language just fell away. I felt no need to express myself so colorfully. In about three months' time I began to realize that I was actually feeling things again. I was beginning to perceive the voice of God. Deep in my inner man I sensed that God was answering some questions. My pastor had changed. I know he did. Somehow I knew that his red-faced, loud responses were no longer expressing anger. Those things were an indication of his passion, his heartfelt response to the stirring of God's voice in his inner man. I don't know why he changed when I did, but somehow it happened. He even asked me to be one of the leaders of the boys' group at the church. I'm still questioning that move. I really wasn't that saved yet. In every contest those boys entered, their attitudes were affected by mine. It was no longer, "It doesn't matter whether we win or lose, it is how we play the game." Nope, can't do that. Now it was, "There is only one reason to enter the game. We play to win!" We did win some contests those two years.

Now, as I look out over those Ozark Mountains, my thinking is no longer challenged by longing to know and understand. I am simply amazed at the handiwork of my Father.

RECKON WHAT WOULD HAPPEN IF...

We sat in the Dairyette parking lot, the front of the car facing the main road through town. A 1964 Dodge two-door was slowly cruising down in the opposite direction. Every few yards a Black Cat firecracker would leave a smoke trail as it was thrown from the driver's side of the old Dodge. You must realize that the old car was not anything a collector would be looking for. It was purchased because it was cheap and it had a big engine. My cousin was driving the Dodge. His brother and I were sitting in the parking lot, observing this obviously criminal act. After watching for a few minutes we saw that he was reaching in the backseat to get to his firecrackers. An idea began to form, not a completely strange thing to us. Actually, we were not even supposed to be together. Our parents had forbidden that because of some rather dangerous ideas that seemed to surface when we were together. Anyway, we came up with a quick plan and pulled slowly out of the parking lot. We knew the other car would circle at the end of town and drive back through.

As was our habit, I hung my left arm out the window, signaling my cousin to stop and talk. His brother was riding as passenger in my car. As the other car pulled up, he handed me a short cigarette he had been smoking. We talked a few minutes about nothing. Then as we drove away I flicked the burning butt into the backseat of the old Dodge. Since this other cousin was into a lot of things he should not be; he was a little paranoid. When that box of firecrackers began to go off, he first accelerated hard, thinking someone was shooting. Then realizing the sparks and smoke were all inside his car, he slammed on the brakes and slid to the side of the road. The driver's door swung open and he ran for cover.

Laughing like a couple of hyenas, we drove up behind him and got all the sparks out of the car seats and told him what had happened. After a few moments of foul language and some half-hearted anger, he began to laugh. He didn't like all those extra holes in the seat of his car, nor the road rash on his knees, but the bottom line was that he liked his brother and me. He could overlook some rather extreme circumstances because we had a real and true relationship. By the way, it didn't hurt that old car much. Actually, it might have added character and made it a bit more attractive.

I've been trying to serve God for a while now. I am really wondering about some folks. It seems like they are the nicest folks until there is any disagreement about God or the Bible. Then they seem to turn downright mean. I know that I am not anywhere near qualified as a teacher or anything like that, but I think I can see the problem. They don't genuinely like each other. That would be easily taken care of, but it seems they just don't know each other outside of the church meeting. Oh, I know they see each other in town and act like they really know each other, but I don't think they do. The smiles seem to be pasted on. The comments seem to be carefully crafted so the conversation can be considered spiritual. It just seems to me they have forgotten that they are family. I read in some of Paul's writings that we all are of the family and household of God. Having been a part of a family for a long time, I know there are some things about family that you just accept. My mom and some of my aunts are never going to agree, but they are family. They just accept the differences and go on about being family. At the end of the day, they like each other. They gripe and at times rage about something the other has said, but they have a family to care for and they come together to do that.

Is there something about the Bible that causes people to dislike one another? I really watch those people. In every situation each person seems to have a desire to be a child of God. In a private situation, each one can talk of their experience with God and get teary eyed about the work of His hand in their life. Why do they feel like they have to be right when they're in public? I've looked in the Bible and tried to figure this out. I think I have an idea. I think folks give the devil credit that he doesn't deserve and completely miss some things he is doing. Just think; what is the most important thing the powers of darkness can accomplish? Wouldn't it be to divide the family of God? Wouldn't that be the most successful thing the devil could do with born-again people? It just seems to me if he could keep us from being a cohesive family unit, then we would never be effective enough to be the church the prophets described.

When all the fireworks were going off in my cousin's car, I'm glad he didn't insist on being right. Our planning the action, my flipping the cigarette, and even our laughing at a potentially dangerous situation definitely gave him room to be angry and stay angry. It wasn't right for us to do that. But he knew us. Something deep in him responded to something deep in us. Even though he was shocked and angry, there was a deeper relationship that caused him to respond to us like family. At that time in our lives none of us were godly. But, in my thinking, I insist that there was something righteous in that whole incident. Any way you define the Greek word that is translated "righteous," you will find the roots buried deeply in right relationships, not just being right.

I know that sometimes I live in a world created in my mind. However, I can't keep myself from imagining what this world would be like if the church would just be a family. Even as I write those words, there is a warm, good feeling that ripples over me. I don't think there is anything in the Bible that supports the lack of family that exists in much of the church world. I'm thinking the whole world would be impressed and deeply affected if we all acted like family. Somehow in my mind I can see results that defy description. What an awesome thing it would be if we lived in a world where we never referred to "those people" in "that church," but instead talked about and with our brothers, sisters, and cousins who are from that branch of the family. Would there be differences? Of course! But just think of the result of this kind of living.

I could ask the questions that I want to ask. And perhaps more to the point, I would not feel like I am automatically coming under verbal fire when I ask! There are things that trouble me. I would like to ask those questions. I have asked some of them and have gotten some amazing answers. Since I was raised in the old Pentecostal tradition, I was taught that people who did not believe this way were off. Some of the preaching even indicated that these other folks might not get their mansion—for me that wasn't a downside. Early in my Christian life I met a man from "that church." He was a pastor of "those people." Somehow he and I became good friends. He was interested in my beliefs, and I was interested in his. We spent hours talking about the Holy Spirit, His expression, and His work among believers. I was thoroughly surprised. We were not far apart in our beliefs. He loved Jesus with all his heart. He was open to anything I could show him in Scripture. Our churches had many times of worship together. Everyone concerned was blessed to find that this was part of the church family. We all wanted to serve God and to live a life unto Him. What a tremendous gift this man gave me in friendship. He allowed me to question without being threatened. He accepted our differences. He was open to learning.

Now, I'm not one that is given to a lot of yelling. I've lived in places where that would get you in a lot of trouble. Since I'm not a yeller, I must admit that I have opinions about those who are. Some of my opinions are questionable. I have been wrong many, many times. When I consider this honestly, then I am less surprised when I am proven wrong again. However, I have gathered from reading the Bible that our words are anointed. Also, there is the suggestion that such gifts from God are never removed from us. For me, I am almost overwhelmed with this responsibility. All of my words will have some effect. If I project them with the force of yelling, then they will have greater effect. I'm guessing that some folks have never considered this. It seems that every time someone questions them, they yell. What is all the yelling about? Why do some get in the pulpit and yell from start to finish? I'm betting it is because they don't realize they are addressing family. I know. That is simplistic, but wouldn't that change the whole thing if we just understood more fully the anointing and the family household of God?

I'm in the navy now and I'm still fascinated by God, although my life don't show it. There is a church group near the base that is being talked about by a lot of the sailors. The people there are at least being nice to the guys that visit. By this time I know that I need God. My wife and I decide to go and check it out. We go inside and are greeted by some nice people. We sit near the back. A few minutes later an older lady walks in, stood beside me, and said, "That is my seat!" I think she is being funny and I look up with a smile. Her response? "It's not funny! That is my seat! You will have to move!" This is my first time in church in over four years. I'm not used to taking a lot of stuff from anybody, but this time I remember that I am in a place where people meet to worship God. I respond, "Okay. We'll move." And we do. Right back down the aisle and out the door. I did not return to church for two years or more.

I understand that my response wasn't the best. I can't help but wonder what would have happened if she had seen us as returning prodigals. How different it could have been if my wife and I had been welcomed as family. We'll never know, but I have also never forgotten that feeling. Angry? Yes, but also deeply disappointed. Even now I realize that I had gone in response to the seeking of the Shepherd. Just deciding to go to church was not something I would have done. Even then He was searching for my lost soul and pulling me to Him.

Even as I write I have a desire to know Him more. Also, a desire to know my brothers and sisters in the family of God even more. How can I be more righteous? My prayer is that God will lead us in this. Reckon what might happen if…?

HE GIVES ME THE SHIVERS!

I'm not a boy anymore, but I guess some of my boyhood will always be with me. My dad always told us that ghosts weren't real, and most of the time that is what I believed. At other times I wasn't sure what I believed. We had an old barn on the north side of the house. It was just far enough from the house to keep the older folks from going there often. It was the work place of the males of the family. Since Mom mostly stayed away, we felt it was a safe place for the guys to go when we had company. We did a lot of things that moms in general just should not be a part of. One of our favorites was to gather in the haystack and tell ghost stories. I had a cousin from Texas who could tell a ghost story in a way that would make us shiver. Problem was, those stories never had an end. He was several years older, and he just walked away with all those ghosts hanging out in our imagination. No end to the story. When he walked away, those of us who were younger just sat with big eyes and even bigger imaginations looking up into the darkness of the rafters of that old barn. It was not airtight, so the wind moved anything that was loose. What had been old burlap bags hanging on nails in the light of day became ghostly possibilities as they blew in the soft winds of the night. In the light of day that wind was a comforting sound as it whistled and moaned through the old barn, but late at night we weren't certain if it was only the wind or not. At those times ghosts seemed a lot more real than when Dad confidently asserted, "That's a bunch of bull! Ghosts ain't real!"

I went to high school with a guy who was a little bit "spooky" on any day. Everyone liked him, but he was very easily scared. Folks from Oklahoma know why I stated it that way. The contradiction in that statement is that a lot of us won't waste any of our "liking" on those males who admit they are spooky. This wasn't a mean streak or anything. It's a simple entertainment issue. It is a lot more fun to scare a person who isn't known as "spooky." That is why my high school friend was unusual. He had a lot of personality *and* a fastback Torino with a 429, four-speed manual transmission. *That* is a likeable combination for nearly anyone. Just outside Vinita is a cemetery that the guys liked to drive through on Saturday nights. Rumor had it that ghosts had actually been seen while driving through slowly with headlights off on a moonlit night. Again, it was simple entertainment. The girls sitting at our side would cuddle up real close as we slowly drove through that cemetery. And drove slowly through the cemetery. And drove slowly through the cemetery.

As I'm thinking of ghosts—of course they don't exist—one night in particular stands out to me. Three friends and I were standing in a parking lot, leaning against our cars, and talking to our friend with the Torino. All of us were known more for what we drove than who we were. Our friend was sitting in his car with his girl next to him on the bench seat. Bench seats were also a desirable thing, especially with a manual shifter coming up out of the floor. Anyway, we were talking about that cemetery. The three of us had been together in so many pranks that we just automatically thought in the same ornery patterns. Matter of fact, in those days that was about the only pattern to our thinking. When one of us brought up the cemetery all of us began the setup. As the stories of ghosts got bigger and bigger, even a little bit believable, the girl in the Torino started to get interested. Without even talking it over, we had a plan. We would get them hooked with stories, and sooner or later that night they would go drive through that cemetery.

Well, it worked better than we thought. On the road through the cemetery there was a tree with a limb that hung out over the road. It was a large limb with a lot of leaves and not very high off the road. We drove out and parked in the dark behind the old church building. Two of us hid behind larger grave stones, and one climbed the tree and shinnied out on that limb. It was perfect. We could hardly see him with a flashlight. We didn't have long to wait. We saw the lights in the distance. Soon that Torino slipped apprehensively into the cemetery road. With a short pause at the start of the road, they drove slowly toward the limb. The only thing we had forgotten was how powerful the engine was in that Torino. As the car moved under the limb our friend dropped off that limb onto the top of the Torino. Was he ever in for a ride. With a roar that only a big-block Ford can make, that car was off down the road and he was holding on for dear life. Luckily there was a hard right turn out of the cemetery. He was tossed head over heels into the ditch, leaving clearly defined fingerprints on the top of the Torino. We could hear that car going through the gears all the way to the highway and back into town. It was years before we ever admitted we had been in the cemetery that night and have yet to tell the owner of the Torino!

Maybe through all this you can understand why it's a bit of a struggle for a guy like me when the pastor starts talking about the Holy Ghost. That's right. All the pastors and teachers call Him a ghost. There is a bit of a war going on in my thinking. On the one hand, I'm almost certain I want to get involved and experience what they are talking about. On the other hand, I have been a part of making people believe something when it is not true. Not that I thought they were lying. Not at all. But I have seen people begin to believe in ghosts when, in truth, they had been set up. And I had been witnessing—that's a fancy church word used for watching. It's much more acceptable than peeking and don't get you in near as much trouble. Anyway, I had seen folks react in ways that leave me wondering. It seems to me they get the "shivers." I remember those days of sitting in the barn. I was shivering inside and doing my best not to show it. I didn't want to be known as "spooky." I remember the feeling I had when my friend dropped out of that tree. I was yards away and I still felt a shiver go through me. The feeling I had when those people reacted in unusual ways made me feel the same way. I was all "shivery" and usually just wanting to be anywhere else and not in that place.

Somehow, I was still drawn to it all. So, as was my habit by now, I began to look in the Bible. I read everything I could find about this *Holy* Ghost. It wasn't long before I realized that most folks wrote about the Holy Spirit and left out the "ghost" part. I'm still not certain why, but that made me feel better automatically. I read things like, "Now, the Lord is the Spirit." Well, that makes sense to me. Our Lord and Savior, Jesus, died, rose again, and went to be with our Father. Seems to be okay for His main representative on this earth to be

His own Spirit. From the beginning I'm glad I can't understand it all completely. I know if I understood it all, I would somehow try to control it. I've found out the hard way that I shouldn't be in full control.

Then I find some other things. Try this one on for size. "Those who are joined to the Spirit are one spirit with Him." In my thinking that shakes up my world. However, in daily practice of life, I begin to understand. I can sense His presence. Not a weird, shaky, shivery feeling, but just a sense of His presence. More than that, I am getting the idea that the Holy Spirit really likes hanging around with me. It seems He is there all the time. I almost don't dare to think like this, but it seems like He is my buddy. I think I sense His humor, His sadness, His worship, His exuberance, and—I know, I think it's a little irreverent too—sometimes, His orneriness! Could it be that He adapts Himself to our personalities so that we can more fully know Him? Even now, I don't know for sure, but I think maybe it is so. Darn it! I hope I'm not missing something important here. With all the awe and reverence I can muster, I begin to think of the Holy Spirit as my friend.

I'm reading about those guys in the Old Testament again. As I read the full stories, I am aware that they are just normal guys. They really are. The Bible is so faithful to record their true lives. Almost all of these guys—David, Samson, Abner, Moses—are so normal. Their personal lives are often a mess, and yet the Holy

Darn It! Maybe I Missed Something!

Spirit comes on them and it all changes. Now, I'm asking myself an entertaining question. What if He really does "come upon" me? Is it possible that I might go down in history as one of those who work together with Him? I still have to deal with some of my old ways of thinking. I'm still ornery to the core. I'm wondering what a supernatural prank might look like. Would the Holy Spirit help me with a joke or two? This brings to mind a friend of mine who is almost as irreverent as me. At a time when he and his wife were having real difficulty, he was driving along, trying to commune with God. He was telling God that if there ever was a time when he needed to hear Him, it was now. With a dark cloud of despair hanging over him, he was almost certain he heard the voice of the Holy Spirit. "Now you know why Jesus never got married!" Now, I feel all the reservations and shock that everyone who reads this will feel. That don't change the fact that my friend had to pull over beside the road and get out of the car and just laugh. It was just what he needed to see clearly and get out of the despair and make necessary choices for his life. Was it the Holy Spirit? Darn it! I might be missing something, but I am leaning toward believing it just might have been Him. He does know what we need and when we need it. If my way of considering Him were to broaden, then it is quite possible that He really would "come on me" in ways I had not previously considered.

WORKING TOGETHER? NOW I CAN DO THAT!

"Get up! Let's get this day done so we can go down to the coal pit." Now, to a lot of people that wouldn't be very exciting. When my dad would say that on a Saturday morning, it caused a flurry of activity in our house. The words *coal pit* meant an entirely different thing to us than it did to most folks. About five hundred yards from our house was an old strip mine. It was filled with some of the clearest water in Oklahoma. The old-timers said it was fed at the bottom by a freshwater spring. That old pit had about everything a family could want in entertainment. On one side was shallow water with a bottom of Oklahoma blue shale, and on the other side was a twelve or fourteen-foot cliff straight into very deep water. Try as we might, none of us ever found the bottom of that pit on the deep side.

Most folks in Oklahoma know that there are some very large cottonmouth water moccasins in that area. One of the first things you check a swimming hole for is snakes. How are the banks? Could one of those big snakes be lurking in the cattails? And, while swimming you keep an eye out for them, too. If you see that rippling of the water that has a slithering motion, you ask no questions. You just get out of the water—very carefully. All the old folks say, "Where there is one there will surely be two." I don't know if that is scientifically correct, but we didn't hang around to check. That old coal pit had special water. There were no snakes in that pit. It was beautifully surrounded by cattails, weeds, and rocks—but no snakes. I had actually seen an old black water snake slither off into it one day. He didn't even get his whole length into it before he was turning around and getting back out.

As you can see, this hole of water was very nearly perfect. We never questioned why those snakes stayed out. There was no fish or turtles either. However, in retrospect it was probably polluted in some way or another. I know for sure that something made all our kids be born naked. Other than that, most of us who swam there were somewhat normal.

I suppose, as I look back, my dad was pretty smart. He didn't get many Saturdays off work, and he wanted to get the most out of that day. On the farm there were a lot of days full of work. Seemed there was always more work than time. We just had to decide how much we would do every day. Or more to the point, Dad had to decide how much we would do each day. He worked in the coal mines and gave us our working orders. We would get it done through the day or face his displeasure—now ain't that a nice word?—when he came home just after dark in the evening. On those Saturdays he just seemed to know he could get more out of us if he worked with us. Especially if we had something set before us. Something like a trip to the coal pit.

As I study all the Bible has to say about the Holy Spirit, I feel like I really understand His intent. He is going to work a lot like my dad. I remember several Saturdays in a row when the coal mine had no contracts. In those times the men only worked five days a week repairing equipment. Dad decided we would build a corral around the barn area on those Saturdays. He had gathered about umpteen-hundred hard oak pallets just for the job. So we began the job. I thought he was the strongest man I had ever seen. We dug postholes big enough for used railroad cross ties. He used an old model A axle to bust through all that sandstone—yes. I know about "bust." At those times it seemed like Oklahoma grew sandstone better than anything else. He would tell us, "Stand clear!" Then he would pick up that crosstie. Up it would go, all the way on his shoulder. Then across the corral, and *thump!* Down into that big hole. Someday I would be just like him. When we nailed those pallets to the crossties, Dad lost some of his godlike qualities. If you've never drove a nail through red oak pallet wood, you have missed a trying experience. Those nails bend like noodles. Fingers get bruised and often bleed. The language isn't exactly godly during those times. Darn it! I'm not missing this. I'm going to talk like him too someday. When he's not listening!

It just seemed like Dad was doing most of the work. Mostly because he could. It seems like it's the same with the Holy Spirit. As I read about what He does it seems like he is going to do the largest portion of it. I still get the "shivers" when I read some of those passages. When the Bible says, "And the Holy Spirit came upon" whoever, I want to shout, "Stand clear!" I just know the Holy Spirit is going to do something, and most folks will be looking at the human part of that and thinking, "How did he do that?" There is this awesome, wonderful, and humbling aspect to working with the Holy Spirit. I can almost feel the wonder with which Paul spoke the words that were written, "And being workers together with Him…" He works with us, and in many ways it looks like we have accomplished the work. I remember how proud I was when we finished that corral. It felt like I had done the whole thing. We stepped back and took a look. I knew that all I had done was drag the pallets out of the pile and over to the fence. I had pulled out nails with names—I had heard Dad name them. To his credit he gave most of them the same name. I had carried water, but when we were finished, it felt like I had done the whole thing!

The Holy Spirit is like that. He trained David's hands for war. He "came upon" Samson many times. He spoke through His prophets. I'm thinking He did most of the work. For me, the most amazing thing is that He lets me help. I know it's not always easy for Him. I must get in the way a lot. I remember when I got too ambitious helping build the corral. That big hand grabbed whatever was convenient and pulled, pushed, or whatever to get me out of the way. It makes me smile when I think of God moving me to the side. I'm sure there are times when He just needs to get it done; even so, He does let me help.

I looked up the word that has been translated Comforter. Now He is that more often than not. I know that part of Him well. But there is much more to it than that. *Parakletos*. When I saw that I knew there must be something I was missing. Darn it! I'm glad I didn't just put the Holy Spirit in some kind of a comforting box and leave Him there. There is not much in that box to encourage a country boy like me to hang out there. But I found a much more likely story—God just has to be bigger than we have allowed Him to be.

What I found out was that Roman soldiers always fought in pairs. Now, this came from a university teacher in Greece. The older, more accomplished soldier would take the younger soldier, and they would be together throughout their service. Even while resting, they were together. The younger would serve the older, but in battle they would be side by side. If an enemy approached from the back, they fought back-to-back. If the younger was wounded, the older carried him back to camp and nursed him to health. Very often these men would even be together in retirement. They were simply inseparable. In historic accounts this was often missed because it was so commonplace.

I can only imagine how scary battle was in those days. A young and untried soldier must have gone through some real fear. I know from experience that a soldier is not usually afraid of whether or not he will run. He is afraid of his lack of ability until that ability is tested. For a young soldier who would fight with sword and spear, this was reality. I just don't see any way to know if a soldier is good enough until he hears the clang of metal striking metal. He cannot know for certain until the enemy is defeated. How comforting it must have been to the young soldier to see the battle-scarred, hard but confident visage of the older soldier. I'm betting he was glad that older soldier was there. No matter if he was a hard taskmaster. Who knows the depth of discipline needed to win better than an old soldier?

Darn It! Maybe I Missed Something!

Concerning the Holy Spirit, I'm just glad He is here with us. As we move ahead spiritually, we have no way to know what is ahead. Reading the record of those gone before in the Bible, I recognize that they, too, knew what it was to need a comforter. Gideon was hiding out behind a wine press when the Holy Spirit started talking to him. Talked 'ole Gideon right into victory. About the time those lamps broke and the trumpets blew, I bet Gideon was needing a little comforting. *Parakletos.* No doubt I am missing a lot of things, but I can sense the hand of the Holy Spirit on my shoulder. It's like we are looking back at some of the things that have been accomplished. I am so blessed to have been a part of those things. I didn't do much but drag around a few spiritual pallets, but somehow I feel like I've had a part. Then as He and I take a look at the present, I think I can work with Him on it. I'm sure going to need His help. I don't know how to do any of this stuff on my own. I can't dig those holes. I can't lift those ties. I can keep Him company, and if He needs any ice water...

I'm also blessed to have found that there are a few spiritual "coal pits" out there. As life goes on I find there are blessings that I had no part in. None of my family worked in that particular strip mine, but we did get the blessing for many years. After a hard day's work we could dive, swim, play, and splash until well after dark. We didn't have to worry about snakes, there weren't any. Some times are like that in God. We just play in the blessing. We can relax and enjoy His presence, His pleasure, and His blessing. It was not about earning a time of play. It was about getting a job done and then enjoying each other. I sincerely hope that Christians everywhere learn to just enjoy Him. Not just in the play, but also in the work. Just when it seems we cannot get the job done, we sense that mighty hand reaching into our world and accomplishing the task. This is worship. Giving Him worth in everything I do, everything I say, and seeing His hand at work in all of my world.

I'VE BEEN AFRAID TO ASK THESE QUESTIONS!

Some things are not about being rebellious or about being country folks, but are more about who you are. Christmas was a big event in my life because we got to go to Granny and Granddad's house. We went at other times, but at Christmas all the cousins, aunts, and uncles were there. That little old house was packed to the busting point with people who genuinely liked each other. At the Easter reunion earlier in the year, all of us drew names, and there were presents everywhere. None of us had a lot of money, so we didn't spend a lot of money. All of us took the time to try to make the gift match up with the personality of the person we were giving it to. It was a fun time of receiving things like trucks, tractors, cowboy hats, and I suppose a few dolls. Those never caught my attention, so I can't say for sure.

Even though it was many years ago, I can still remember one of those Christmas reunions. Everyone was gathered around opening gifts. All the kids were in great anticipation. Finally, my name was called. I took the gift to the side and opened it. There, in all its glory, was a necktie. I smiled and said thank you as I should have done. But inside was the most disappointment I had ever experienced in all of my five long years. I knew I didn't dare to ask the question. It just wasn't allowed to be unthankful even in private. But, inside I wondered, *Why would anyone buy me a necktie?* Had they gotten me mixed up with someone else? No. It was a very short, clip-on tie. All the other guys seemed quite happy with what they had gotten. Everyone else seemed to have been matched up quite well. So I had a tie and no shirts with collars. I was thankful for one thing. I knew my dad would not make me wear it. He wasn't mean or anything.

That same kind of question comes to me as I try to find my way among church people. I know I am called to minister. I've wrestled with that for several years, but by now I know. I just know that I know. I've been preparing through study, even doing some mild teaching things from time to time. But I'm troubled. I'm afraid to ask some of the questions that I have. I don't want to be seen as rebellious or disrespectful.

Darn It! Maybe I Missed Something!

Also, previous teaching has made me quite fearful of "touching God's anointed." Seems kind of like a shelter of some kind, if you ask me. I know. No one asked. But it seems like a sure-fire way to keep anyone from asking questions. What if God really meant it that way? What if by questioning I "touch" something He has said not to touch?

But, I'm dealing with that thinking problem again. That thing that sends me to the Bible to see if I am in danger or what. Darn it! I just might be missing something, but I'm learning things about the Holy Spirit that make me think that He really knows me. Oh, my goodness! While I was in my mother's womb, He knew me. All of my days were numbered. All those things that I used to do? He knows all about them. Whew! I'm thinking we better change the subject. I don't want to remind Him. We're getting along pretty good. I am so thankful for His forgetfulness. Now, that makes me chuckle. My grandfather, on my dad's side, now he had some forgetfulness. I knew him and loved him. He was one of my favorite people. He was hard to get along with sometimes, but most times he liked us kids. But he could forget! One of the granddaughters was trying to find his BB gun—the one he shot dogs with when they got in his tomato plants. She thought she could put it away where he couldn't find it. Then the neighbors wouldn't call the cops. He forgot where he put it. Could not remember. Then it appeared like magic when those dogs trotted down the sidewalk. One of the grandkids asked him once, "Papa. What do you think God would think of you shooting those dogs?" His reply? "He'd think I was a pretty good shot, wouldn't He?" Yep. I really loved that old man. But I'm not a bit like him. Nope.

Anyway, I've come to know God well enough to ask Him some questions. I know He is forgetful enough that He is still talking to me. My questions sometimes come as querying statements. I don't know where I got that word *querying*. Probably in Oklahoma English class. Anyhow, I became bold enough to ask, "God, why do all these guys wear suits?" I really wanted to know. I don't think God answered me on a question-by-question basis. I'm pretty sure He was embarrassed to answer. He didn't want all those ill-fitting suits and ties blamed on Him. I can understand that.

I've heard all the arguments about wearing the best you have. But don't that depend on what "best" means? Or something like that. In my growing up years my "best" would never have been a suit, tie, and low-cut shoes. It wouldn't even have been on my shopping list if I had a lot of money—which was never a problem. My "best" was my best pair of Levis, my newest western shirt, and my dress boots—which would become my work boots as they wore out. In my opinion that was not only my best, but the way that I looked the best. The two or three times I wore a suit in those days

Darn It! Maybe I Missed Something!

I was embarrassed to look in the mirror. I honestly thought I looked like a sissy boy, and I knew I was not that.

I asked Him about all of it. Speaking my mind into His thundering silence. *God, what about that hairdo?* In my life hair was something to be combed out of your way or tucked up under a hat. I had no need of hairspray, razor cuts, or even razors for that matter. And, "God, those shoes. Oh, Lord. How would I ever get anywhere in Oklahoma with low-cut shoes? All those blackberry bushes, chiggers, and worse? But, God, that really don't bother me all that much when I compare those to all the plastic relationships. I'm going to some of those meetings! It's, 'Hello, Doc' to my face, and 'Who in the world is that?' when I'm gone. Surely, God, there is more to this walk with You." I have access to some of those guys. I'm going to talk with some of them. Darn it! Maybe I'm missing something again!

I talked with some really big names in my area, and I am sick at heart. I know they are difficult, arrogant people in their private lives. I've asked some of them to talk to me about things and have been told they don't have the time. Or worse, they just ignored me. But when I see them in the pulpit, I am amazed. Everything changes. They are everybody's friend. By their own declaration they are moved with compassion. I heard them say it. A few minutes before they couldn't say hello. They only looked down their super spiritual noses at a young man in new Levis, new boots, and a good shirt. The problem was, I really needed to talk to some of those people. I had real needs that couldn't be covered up by a suit. I needed, *needed*, answers by this time. I thought people who had such a good reputation could help me. My young wife was ill with a disease that would eventually take her life. I was hurting. My family was hurting. I felt faithless.

Then I ran across some real people and I realized that here was God's answer to me. I saw a name in a denominational flyer that caught my attention. This was a missionary that my family had known well. I went to those meetings and identified myself to this man. He took time at breakfast the next morning to talk with me at length. He told me of his own life traveling to Africa and back to the States, often many times every year. He told me of losing his seventeen-year-old son in an auto accident while he was away. His own wife had been ill for many years and had to stay in the States while he was in Africa. However, those were not the things he dwelled on. Those were things I picked up while he was glorifying his Lord and Savior and speaking of the magnificent things he had witnessed as he lived life with the Holy Spirit.

Beginning with this man, I heard the voice of God answering my questions. He had known who I was when He saved me. He knew I would never be a man to push myself forward or to demand things from

Darn It! Maybe I Missed Something!

Him. He knew I would never be listed in the fashion magazines—I am in style about every fifteen years. That's about how long it takes to come around again. Seriously, He knew me. In His gifts for me there would never be a necktie. I would wear one occasionally, but it would have come from a real snazzy store like J.C. Penney's or somewhere. It would be for an occasion where someone required it of me, but not Him. No sir! He likes my boots. I'm sure glad because my feet are kind of formed to them now. When I die my foot will look like a boot with a walking heel.

All the opinions I had stated to God about those other men? Those were my opinions, not God's. I've come to realize that in my own way I am as snooty as any of them. I still cannot get it in my head that a suit looks good. Now, a nicely cut western jacket? Along with some Wrangler dress slacks? And a pair of Tony Lama's? Now that is dressing! Fit to kill! Although it is difficult for a guy like me, I can even see where God would use the other kind occasionally. After all, He is God. He can do what He wants. But I am blessed. He likes me, and there are things about me He doesn't want to change. He don't even try.

I am amazed to realize that He welcomed the questions. He answered them over time through life experience. He welcomed the quest as much as the questions. Through our questions we begin a quest that leads us into more and more knowledge of God.

But, even more precious to me, through the quest for faith, for His person, God brought me into relationship with some of the most real and true people on the face of the earth. How I value those lives! How I look forward to spending eternity with them. We will always be together in our quest to know Him and on a journey of discovery of our Savior and Lord.

I KNOW HIM. HE'S MY FATHER!

"I can always tell who is coming up out of the pit. He makes that old truck sound like an automatic transmission." My heart swelled with pride as my coworker made that comment on that cold Oklahoma morning. I was working as a part of the blasting crew. This was a man who had worked with my dad for many years. His comment was an observation, but I took it personal. My dad was one of the best drivers in the history of that company. I was very glad that someone knew it. Many days through my growing-up years, I spent the entire day in the cab of one of those old White Freightliners. I was truly "endangered" as a child and didn't even know it. What if that old truck had somehow tumbled off down into that coal pit? Well, in our thinking, that could not happen. Dad was driving. All was well.

I was blessed with one of the greatest gifts a boy could ever have. I had a dad who was larger than life all his years. As I look back, I know that I would have said the same thing if you had asked me even as a child. My dad had to work long, hard hours. Most weeks he had no time at home that could be termed "quality" time. With few exceptions, he got up at four thirty a.m., left for work after a quick breakfast, came home about forty-five minutes after dark, ate supper, washed the coal dust off himself, and dropped into bed to sleep. Yet we knew him. I lived for those evenings when I would hear that old pickup truck's loud exhaust as he slowed to turn off Highway 66 onto the road to our house. I would quickly finish whatever I was doing and meet him in the barnyard where he parked the truck. My younger brother was usually right behind me. Dad would pick up my brother and lift him to his shoulders, throw his arm around mine, and off we would go. Home was never what it should be until he got there. We all knew that supper was waiting—not dinner. We ate that at noon. Some folks are a bit mixed up on that, but we knew what to expect. As my brother was swung to the floor and I stepped aside so Dad could take off his boots, the whole atmosphere of that house changed. Daddy was home. He never failed to touch my sister's shoulder as he walked past, headed to the bathroom to wash the grease and coal dust off his hands. "Hi, sis. Doin' okay?" Most days he sat at the table with his hands clean up to the elbow and his face washed. The rest of him was covered in diesel and coal dust. None of us have ever forgotten that smell. Diesel, coal, our dad.

Now our dad wasn't a perfect man. But, as I said before, he was larger than life. The imperfections could not overpower that absolute fact. He was our father in the best sense of the word. None of us had come into this family by accident or without a welcome. This man had always wanted family. By his own admission, he could have never been happy without us. I know as I look back that our family was what completed him as a man. Dad was an unusual man in many ways. He loved to work. Always, in his thinking, there was some plan to make the farm a better place for his family. Most likely he would never have been able to express himself in those terms, but his life and his actions declared those facts. He gave us the values that all of us have carried into life. It was something special to stand back with Dad and look at a day's work. When you work with your hands, there is a feeling of having accomplished something. It is a good feeling.

While growing up I wondered why young people liked to hang out at our house. After many years I can look back and fully understand. Those kids knew my dad's schedule better than I did. All of them knew what time he went to bed and what time he came home. It was very normal for some old cars to show up right about the time the old truck roared into the barnyard. They weren't a part of the family ritual of greeting, but they never failed to get a warm smile of greeting or a hard bump on the shoulder, whatever fit. They knew they were welcome. The family went on just the same, but they were included. They were welcome to supper or just to sit and be a part. Dad loved to laugh and joke. He laughed when some church folks thought he should have joined them in their "pinched look" responses at times. As I look at it all now, I know that it wasn't the food or the laughter, it was the man. He simply liked people. He enjoyed life and was eager to share it with others.

I guess that is why it wasn't difficult for me to begin to understand my heavenly Father. While I don't want to be irreverent or cause anyone to bring God to a lower level, I can see that in many ways God is like my dad. He probably don't name so many nails, nor talk to cattle in the same way as Dad, but knowing my dad helps me to know God. I am so sorry for people who cannot make the comparison. Oh well, maybe I can help those people to have a comparison by the way I live.

I don't remember a time in my life that I was embarrassed to introduce my dad. I never said formally, "This is Clel Berry." It was always, "This is my dad." I was not ever proud to be me. I'm still not, but I am comfortable with being me. But, was I ever proud of my dad! On the rare occasion that dad would visit the school, I walked right beside him. I wanted people to know. This was my dad. He was here because of me. Never, ever, did he have to visit school because of my bad behavior. I did act up some. But I took the consequences and changed my behavior enough so that he would not need to visit. One of *those* visits would not have been healthy for me. I was well aware of what he was capable of when punishment was in order. He did not like to do that. When he felt it was necessary, he made a lasting impression. None of us would cause that to happen on purpose.

I remember some of the boys on the playground. When they would get into a fight, it would always be the same thing. "I'm going to tell my dad!" "My dad will beat your dad." "My dad is bigger." I knew there was no need for me to say things like that. My dad would not settle day-to-day arguments for me. I can only imagine how angry he would be if I asked him to do that. Some things were of my own making. I needed to work them out. He had enough problems. He wanted me to learn to handle things on my own. If I got beat up at school, he only had one question. "What did the other guy look like?" It wasn't about who won, but it was about whether or not I was in the fight. I would never have told him that I didn't respond to being punched. My answer was usually, "Not too good." End of conversation. Dad knew I was in the game. It was enough. However, if he ever heard that I started a fight, the whole thing changed. I never did that. I knew him well enough to know the outcome, and I didn't like it. I would have had to apologize to whoever I had picked a fight with. It was the rules of the game.

As the Bible opened up to me, it was so easy for me to slip into the idea that God wanted to be known as Father. He had worked in other times and seasons in many ways, but in these days that I live in His desire is to work as Father. He had given His only natural-born Son so that we could know Him in this way. I suppose I will never be able to grasp all that, but if that is what God wants, then I'll settle in and try to know Him. Father! Darn it! I might miss a lot of things, but I'm not going to miss out on that. Just the fact that He welcomes me that way seems to demand that I come to Him like that. I'm not so proud of who I am, but have you met my Father, my spiritual Dad? David made some statements that make me think he knew God in that way. I don't think it was just empty words when David wrote, "*My* Lord, and *my* God!" I can't help but chuckle when Jesus tells some religious folks, "Your father is the devil!" He said it! Read it for yourself. Isn't that kind of like, "My Dad is bigger than your dad!?" It might be just the country boy in me, the disrespectful one, but I think that is exactly what He was saying.

My goodness! I know it ain't much, but, "my goodness!" The God of the whole world wants me to know He is a Father to me. He brought me forth because He wants a family. While He is complete in Himself, He chooses to live in family and He wants to adopt me into that. Now if that don't mess with your thinking, try this one on for size. I'm gonna be like Him. Oh, I know. I'm not going to be Him. Of course not. I'm going to be *like* Him. Every step further into His will and way makes me more like Him. We have His full expression of what is pleasing to Him. We have the recording of the life of His Son. We see how a man would live if he follows the Spirit. We are told, "Follow me! And I will make you...," and "All who believe have the right to become sons of God."

Now, I will tell you right now that our Father has more faith than me. Yep. Sure does. I can't see myself like He sees me. But, I'm coming to know Him. I know He brought me forth into this walk with Him. I am proud to call Him Father. I love Him. I like to be around Him. I notice that others are drawn to our relationship. I notice that the more I am like Him the more people are drawn to Him.

He likes me. Our Father likes me. When I focus on my problems, I am prone to separate myself from Him. But when I look for Him, He hasn't moved at all. When I run to meet Him, I can feel His arm thrown around me. Now, I know some of you think that is a bit far out, but just leave me alone. I am enjoying this walk with God. Oh and don't forget we are family. You might not agree with me, but you are stuck with me. We will spend eternity getting to know our Father. We will agree and disagree, but we will still be family. We might need to overlook some things so we can do good for the family. Darn it! I must be missing something! Could you lead me into some more knowledge of our Father? I really welcome you into this walk with us. Me and my heavenly Dad.

I AM AMAZED!

As my three-year-old goes flying down the slope of the driveway, I am watching with a completely new sense of wonder. Our daughter has ridden this Big Wheel trike so much that all three tires are so thin you could put a finger through them. The trike is a large plastic contraption that has hidden abilities. If a child rides this thing just right, it can be made to do things that just don't seem possible. The only brakes on the thing are hand brakes beside the rider's seat on each side. This particular driveway slants down toward the house, goes all the way through the carport, and then a sidewalk runs alongside the carport all the way to the storage shed in back. At three years old, this child of ours has learned to start at the top of the drive, pedal as hard as she can, grab the right brake, and skid sideways into a right turn, then grab the left brake, and line up down the sidewalk. All of that at top speed, thus the worn plastic wheels.

As I watch her I wonder how many times she smashed into the laundry room at the end of the carport before she learned how to handle those brakes. I know she is doing this for my benefit. That is why I am thinking so hard about this. I have just been studying in an old Bible that has been lying around the house. Honestly, I was studying more in a dictionary than in the Bible. Also, my father-in-law lives just across town. He has this huge set of Bible commentary books. I have been looking at the word *worship*. Somehow I just know that worship must be a lot more than singing in a song service on Sunday morning. If that's it, well that's it, but my mind won't settle down 'til I know.

I have found some amazing things. First of all, the word *worship* in the old English began as *worthship*. Immediately, this had my attention. I was reading that commentary and everything else those books had to offer on worship. Just adding those two letters opened my understanding. I could feel life in the Puritan writings that were included in some of those books in my father-in-law's library. Somewhere in it all I began to get a mental picture—yeah, that is not always good in my case, but this time I think it is okay. There seemed to be a life of worship that most folks were missing. Seems to me that there is a circle of worthship that was applied in those early days. Some of those old writers talked about giving worth to their fellow believers. Others went on and on about worthship as they looked at God's creation with great awe and wonder. Several wrote about our Father giving worthship to men and women who follow Him.

As I watched our daughter whizzing down that driveway at breakneck speed—literally—I was thinking about worthship in our small circle. She was like my shadow in those days. Her mother was already ill and couldn't get around well, so our daughter went everywhere with me, except to work. Even at this early stage in her mother's illness, our daughter has understanding beyond her years. All the questions that are raging in my mind seem to have little effect on her. I struggle with all the 'whys' and am forced to conclude that God is God and it is unlikely that I will ever understand. None of this seems to touch this little girl. It is what it is. She knows she can't go to work with me, so she takes that in stride. But, anywhere else, she is right there attached to everything I do. I have great worth in her life. I am not the model dad.

I did allow her to risk bodily injury on a regular basis. I figured she was a chip off the old block and she was going to do some things with or without my knowledge and supervision. I found most of it amusing anyway, so I didn't interfere much in her antics. I remember one day when I was getting ready for work. I worked nights. She came in sniffling, almost crying. She knew that crying didn't get very far with me—okay, so she needed therapy. We didn't know much about that in those days. Anyway, the neighbor boy who was three years older was reaching through the fence and holding the handles of her trike. She couldn't move it. Would I come and help? Nope. "Break his arm," I said. Away she went. In seconds I heard the most awful howling in the yard. Maybe I better help. She had grabbed his arm with one hand, holding it on her side of the fence. She had a small plastic bat in the other hand and was whaling away at his arm. He was putting up quite a ruckus. I watched for a minute and then helped her turn him loose. She was about four at the time.

Now, I know I'm missing some things. The truth is I only had my life and the lives of my family available for me to think on. I had to come to know God while looking through the eyeglasses that I had. In all this I am thinking about how worship is a complete life matter. I knew about giving great worth to another life. My wife and my daughter had tremendous worth in my life. The way I treated them in response to that worth would either be worthship to them, or my actions would destroy a part of them and deny them what was truly theirs. There was comprehension beginning to slowly dawn in my thinking. If I see worship as just a song service, I'm not even getting close to worshiping God. If I choose certain times like birthdays and anniversaries to give worth to my family and act like a jerk the rest of the time, I would be giving them nothing. In their minds, life with me would have no value.

About this time another part of it touched my heart. Jesus had made it apparent that He thought of us as friends. Now, how would I want friends to approach me? I want to live life with my friends. I do understand that He is God. What an amazing concept. This wonderful being that is God. This Creator whom I cannot even do justice to in my most vivid imaginings. He is inviting me to be His friend. How am I ever going to do that? If I will ever get this life of worship accomplished I am going to have to figure it out. I already know that He wants more than just singing, shouting, and crying. We can't really get to know Him if we are caterwauling all the time. Darn it! I know that is close to irreverence, but if I am missing something about knowing God, I want to address the issues.

Many folks would declare at this point, "I know Him. I wouldn't ask those questions." Well, if you know Him, what is He like? Let's get to the point here. Can you describe Him like you can describe your best friend? Like you can describe your father? I can almost hear physical transmissions grinding as folks shift into reverse. Most of us have no clue. Shouldn't we have a clue? If He is a friend that "sticketh" closer than a brother? The country boy in me sure likes that word. *Sticketh.* Somehow, it seems more of an action word than *sticks.*

You've probably guessed by now that I'm not much of a singer. The Bible says we should make a joyful noise. I do. I get the joy, you get the noise. If singing is all our Savior gets in worship, then He don't get much from me. He gets volume. He gets quantity. I reckon He will need to get His quality singing somewhere else. I do want to give Him more than that. As I ponder these things, I realize that what will really bless Him is my life. It ain't much. I don't have a lot to invest in this deal, but I sense that is what He wants.

As I watched my daughter on the driveway that morning, I was drawing parallels in my mind. She willingly placed her life in my hands. Somehow she sensed the delight that I had in her. She had great worth to me. In a way that is greatly different than my worship toward God, I gave worth to this little girl and her antics, her life. Right then, as a three-year-old, she didn't have much to offer. But she willingly gave what she had. Sometimes she showed off a little because she knew that I was watching. I didn't mind. I valued her ability. I knew she had some things to go through to get to her place in life. I enjoyed the process.

Darn It! Maybe I Missed Something!

It is with great wonder and reverence that I approach this line of thinking before our Father. I do willingly place my life in His hands. What wonder goes through my being as I realize that He does delight in me. The wreck of a life that I offered Him hasn't changed all that much on the outside. Inside? That is a different matter altogether. There is a freshness, a new awareness of life and its possibilities inside of me. More and more every day I am aware of Him as Lord. He is overseeing my life. As I watch my daughter, I can picture Him in the eye of my mind. He just might be squatting under a shade tree too. Maybe whiling away some time as He watches me go about my life. I'm just beginning this new life. I'm well aware that I am getting the best end of this deal. My Savior has offered me so much. I listen to so-called testimonies in church services. People talk about all the things they have given up to serve God. I don't understand. I didn't give up much of anything. I sure don't miss the hangovers. I've been able to quit some things that I couldn't quit before. Nope. Don't understand.

As I've said before, *God* is not a generic term to me. It is the best I can do to wrap all that He is to me in one term. Now, He is not just the God of my dad and mom. Not just the Savior of my grandmother. He is my God. That helps me to understand more fully. When folks gather to sing together, I know that is not all of their worship. It is just the corporate expression of their lives of worship. I see a lot of things in a new light. We have an older woman in our body of believers. She works a big garden every year. That garden has hill after hill of cucumber vines. Early every morning you can count on seeing her sitting in the dirt working those vines (she has bad knees. Can't kneel). Some days I walk out to say, "Howdy." We do that in Oklahoma. It's only time. Then I listen to her for a few minutes. She could go on and on about how God helped her tend her garden. All the while she would be carefully picking those little cucumbers. Only those that were about two to two-an-half inches long. She would literally pick buckets of those small cucumbers. Those cucumbers were her way into the homes and hearts of many of the castoffs in the neighborhood. Armed with quart jars full of those cucumbers made into pickles, she went knocking on doors. "Thought I would stop by and bring you some pickles." I don't know of any doors in that small town that were closed to her. She would hand the pickles to the lady of the house, sit down, and begin to talk of the blessings of God in her life. Before she left, she would ask, "How are things between you and Jesus?" As I look back now, I know she was worshiping. Worshiping while she worked that garden. Worshiping while she canned those pickles. And as much as I know that I also know that God was smiling, watching, and granting her worth as He observed her going about her days. The only thing I'm missing on this is whatever is to come. For now, I'm still offering Him what I have while He observes my antics. I'm certain that He chuckles over some, even though He knows He will have to correct that sooner or later. He is my Lord, my Savior, my God.

THE WAY YOU SEE HIM IS THE WAY YOU WILL SERVE HIM!

How difficult it is for me to express the sense of humility that is in my spirit as I work my way into this chapter. I'm not suggesting that I am always a humble man. While true humility is difficult to define and even more difficult to live out, one certain thing will mark a humble man or woman. They will be teachable. I do try to be that.

My granddad was a man formed in the hard ways of the late 1800s and early 1900s in west Texas. He often chuckled and stated, "If I owned west Texas and hell, I would lease out west Texas and live in hell." However, we all knew that it wasn't Texas that had been the problem. It was the hard times. Granddad's interaction with his grandkids—we weren't grandchildren (my computer is arguing with me)—anyhow, his interaction with us was often marked by the difficulties that had formed his life. In his world, you had to be strong—sometimes headstrong—to survive. He had little patience with weakness in any form. One of his favorite sayings was, "Ain't no such word as cain't." Now that is good Oklahoma/Texas English. Some folks just haven't gotten that far in their studies.

Sometimes Granddad's ways and words were very difficult to understand. "Boy, get back on that horse. Don't let him know you are scared. Get up. Don't even start that crying. I'll give you something to cry about." You get the picture. Slowly, over time, I began to understand. He gave us life as he understood it. He was offering us all the wisdom that he had gleaned from a difficult and colorful life. If we wanted to benefit from relationship with him, we had to take the things that we didn't understand along with the love and wisdom he had to offer. He was approaching life and relationships with the only understanding available to him. What he had to offer in return became some of the most special times of my life. He taught me about horses. This was very important to me, because I loved horses. I learned that a gently broken horse was more willing to learn than one that was abused into submission. He helped me work my favorite horse until I could do almost anything with him. That horse would not allow just anyone to ride him. He wasn't mean; he just wouldn't do what they asked of him. But for me, he would do almost anything I asked. That horse and I were buddies. Granddad taught me how to do that. Much to my mom's consternation, he taught me to roll cigarettes. He didn't allow me to smoke them in his presence, but I asked how he did it, and he showed me. Those cigarettes brought him great comfort and relaxation. He was sharing what he knew. Oh well!

I think that most folks who know God are like that. Why can't we understand that the lives of the old folks were much different than ours? They learned to know God in a much different school than we did. Many of them led harsh, demanding lives. Their parents were harsh, demanding people who taught their children what life demanded. As a result, the God they knew was often a harsh one. In their own lives they really didn't know how to express the love they had for their children. Their God would be much like that. They wouldn't expect much from Him. As I lived life with those folks, I was amazed by how complicated their lives were before. Just staying alive and providing for their families was a challenge. Slowly but surely I was able to appreciate what they had to offer. They were not mean and interfering people. They truly loved Jesus. Their life had been so hard they looked to Him as Savior and Deliverer. No one ever told them that He was a Father to them as well. For most of them their deliverance is a reality. I'm sure they are learning more about Him as Father and Friend as they venture on into eternity.

I'm sure He understands. As He gets more and more involved in our lives, how it must grieve Him that we don't take time to just discover Him. But I am certain that it doesn't surprise Him. He seems to know the needs we have even before we ask or even think about it. I can only imagine how our Father must treasure the passing of those old folks. His welcome as they enter into the fullness of life with Him would be a pure pleasure to behold. How those folks must live in wonder and awe as they realize who He really is. In my thinking that is why He needs to wipe tears from their eyes. I don't think they are grieving over things. I think they might allow a tear or two to escape as they experience the sheer joy of discovery. Some of them might cry a little in happiness when they discover they don't have to live in a mansion made of gold and silver. They couldn't even hang any pictures on those walls. Nails would surely bend if they tried. Some folks I have known would surely be happy to find they didn't have to live in one of those.

I read in one of the psalms that our Father remembers that we are but dust. Another place says that He remembers that He is our Father. When I pull those two together, I find myself worshiping. As He observes some of my antics, He remembers that He had a part

PHOTO GALLERY

Picture day at school meant keeping your clothes neat
and your hair combed just right "or else."

Glenn Berry

As a boy I spent hours beside the creek watching the fish, small animals, and nature in general.

Darn It! Maybe I Missed Something!

Lots of chores to do on the farm and not all are tough,
Glenn with younger brother Joe.

This is the kind of chore you don't mind so much,
Glenn with younger brother Joe.

This horse and I were buddies,
Glenn with favorite horse, Champ.

Granddad taught me everything
I knew about training horses.

Darn It! Maybe I Missed Something!

Yep, this is the horse that "pulled" me in the wagon that day we ended up in the persimmon sprouts.

Senior Picture, Graduation 1972,
Vinita, Oklahoma

Glenn Berry

United States Navy Basic Training Graduation, 1972

I still look pretty young and harmless here, don't I?
Well, don't be fooled.

There's a lotta folks who'll recognize this guy from back in the day. Lots of fun and lots of trouble.

My late wife, Diana, carried this picture in her Bible until her death from cancer in 2003. She called it her B.C. picture (before Christ).

Despite my wild side, family has always been very important to me. My late wife, Diana, and our 2-month-old daughter, Lesli.

Our Li'l Daredevil, Lesli at about 3 years old.